Relative Wage Differentials in Canadian Industries

Pradeep Kumar

Published by
Industrial Relations Centre
Queen's University at Kingston, Canada

AF738053

1974
Research and Current Issues Series No. 25

© 1975, Industrial Relations Centre
ISBN: 0-88886-060-9

Contents

List of Tables

Preface

The purpose of this study is to explain why some industries pay a higher wage than others to workers of similar skill. It examines whether inter-industry differentials in money wage rates compensate for the differences in non-pecuniary aspects of employment, whether wages are higher in unionized industries than in non-unionized industries, whether large firms pay a wage premium to both skilled and unskilled workers or only to skilled workers, and whether unions are more effective in industries where large firms account for a significant proportion of total employment and output than in competitive industries. The study relates to the differentials among 26 Canadian manufacturing industries in hourly wage rates of unskilled labourers, and also to the differentials in hourly wage rates of skilled maintenance mechanics.

Significance of the Study and Its Relationship to Previous Research

A great deal of research has been done on inter-industry wage differentials, some supporting the competitive theory of the labour market, others raising doubts about the effectiveness of market forces in equalizing returns to labour of similar skills on the grounds that the market in question is not competitive but rather is dominated by organized labour and/or organized management.[1] The results of this research have not been entirely conclusive for three major reasons: a tendency to abstract from the differences in non-pecuniary aspects of employment, disagreement over the possible influence of unions and large firms on relative wage rates, and the use of average hourly earnings — a measure of gross earnings affected, among other things, by the variations in skill mix across industries — rather than occupational-specific wage data. This

1 For a review of this work see M. W. Reder, "Wage Differentials: Theory and Measurement," in *Aspects of Labour Economics* (Princeton: Princeton University Press, published for the National Bureau of Economic Research, 1962).

study attempts to fill these gaps. It endeavours to reconcile the competitive theory of the labour market, which emphasizes the equality of "net advantages" across industries and relates the long run differentials in money wage rates to the compensating differences in non-pecuniary attributes of employment, with the institutional model, which stresses the significant role of trade unions and large oligopolistic firms in relative wage determination. The analytical framework used in this study outlines the significance of both non-pecuniary aspects of employment and institutional factors for the explanation of inter-industry wage differentials, and indicates the interrelationship between the extent of unionization and the degree of large firm concentration in the product market, and between the internal wage structure and the external wage structure.[2] In the empirical test of the model, this study uses occupational wage data rather than average hourly earnings of all production workers.

Outline of the Study

The first chapter reviews the competitive theory of the labour market and the institutional approach to relative wage determination, together with a brief discussion of some of the recent modifications which have helped in providing a rough consensus on the basic elements of an integrated theory of wage determination. The review distinguishes between the assumptions, which have been misused by critics to cast doubts on the validity of the competitive theory, and the predictions of the competitive theory regarding the inter-industry differentials in wage rates for a homogeneous grade of labour. It emphasizes the relevance of non-pecuniary aspects of employment in explaining wage differentials. In the discussion of the institutional approach to wage determination, the review critically examines the nature and the mechanism of union influence on relative wage rates, the rationale behind a wage premium in large firms, and the relationship between unionization and the structure of the product market. It analyzes the three recent modifications to the theory of wage structure, namely the skilled worker hypothesis, the spillover hypothesis, and the manpower flow model, which in one way

2 This interrelationship is considered essential for linking wage theory with the theory of wage structure. See J. T. Dunlop, "The Task of Contemporary Wage Theory," in *The Theory of Wage Determination* (London: Macmillan, 1957), pp. 3-27. Dunlop believes that wage theory must operate with the concept of wage structure and that the central problem of wage analysis is to indicate the interrelationship between the internal and external wage srtuctures.

or the other have attempted to improve upon and helped to integrate the competitive theory and the institutional approach.

The second chapter analyzes the differentials in wage rates among 26 Canadian manufacturing industries for unskilled labourers on the one hand and for maintenance mechanics on the other. These two occupations are singled out for the study partly because they are common to most manufacturing industries and partly because of the availability of wage data. The wage rates of unskilled labourers are correlated with wage rates of maintenance mechanics and with average hourly earnings of all production workers to explore whether some industries pay higher wages to all workers irrespective of their skill or only to workers of particular skill. The relationship between wage levels and wage supplements is also investigated to determine if the differences in wage rates indicate inter-industry differentials in total monetary returns to labour generally.

The third chapter empirically examines the major determinants of inter-industry wage structure in Canada. It outlines an integrated model of relative wage determination in which wage rates for workers of equal skill are determined by differences in non-pecuniary attributes of employment, extent of unionization and the degree of large firm concentration in the product market. Following Adam Smith's *Wealth of Nations*, five non-pecuniary factors are selected for analysis. They are arduousness of work, physical hazardousness, locational mix and the seasonal and cyclical instability in employment. It is argued that relative wage rates are high in those industries where work is more arduous, hazardous, seasonal and cyclically instable, and in industries located in the high wage provinces of Ontario and British Columbia as contrasted with the Atlantic Provinces and Quebec. With regard to the institutional influence on relative wage rates the model postulates that unions have no effect on the relative wage rates for skilled labour. They do, however, raise wage rates for unskilled labour in oligopolistic industries, where a few large firms account for a major proportion of total employment and output. These firms pay a wage premium to skilled workers for greater selectivity in recruiting and for stable attachment, and by insisting upon equitable internal wage differentials, the unions obtain a somewhat similar premium for unskilled workers. It is maintained that because of the unions' policy of equitable occupational wage relationship, the percentage differentials in wage rates of skilled and unskilled workers are lower in unionized industries than in non-unionized industries.

In Chapter 4, the results of the study are summarized together with their theoretical and policy implications.

Limitations of the Study

Like many other studies, the theoretical and empirical value of this study is limited by its scope and the simplifications in the use of data. Some of these limitations can be explicitly stated.

The study relates to 26 industries in the manufacturing sector. Because the industries account for nearly two-thirds of total manufacturing employment, the results can almost certainly be generalized for the manufacturing sector, but may perhaps not be applicable to the non-manufacturing sector.

The study is mainly concerned with the long run determination of relative wage rates for workers of equal skill. It does not investigate the behaviour of inter-industry wage differentials in the short run or the relationship between the structure of wage rates and the general wage level.

Because of its preoccupation with long run static wage determination, any effects of the minimum wage on the wage rates for unskilled workers are ignored. The omission is due to the near unanimity in the literature that the effects of a statutory minimum wage on the wage structure are mostly short run.

The study does not take account of the growing proportion of the cost of employee benefits in total compensation, except for a somewhat brief investigation of their possible effects on the wage structure. The neglect is due to the lack of data.

The study also does not take account of possible differentials in wage rates for workers of equal skill because of the differences in such personal characteristics as age, schooling, and experience. The omission, primarily due to lack of data, is not likely to have any effect on the results pertaining to unskilled workers whose job specifications do not require any formal or informal training, previous experience or the exercise of independent judgement.[3] Although not very likely, wage rates for maintenance mechanics may be slightly higher in some industries than others because of differences in age, schooling and experience. Since these differences are not correlated with industry characteristics their exclusion would not affect the results of this study.

---

3 See *Dictionary of Occupational Titles*, Vol II (Washington: United States Government Printing Office, 1949), p. 319. Until very recently the Canadian classification of occupations was based on this dictionary. The 1961 census of Canada showed that only one quarter of the total unskilled labour force in Canada had more than an elementary education, and their average annual earnings by age did not differ by more than 5 per cent. See *Census of Canada*, Vol. 4.1 (Ottawa: Queen's Printer, 1965), p. B6-29.

Acknowledgements

I am indebted to many people who have kindly and generously helped me in the completion of this study, which was accepted as a doctoral dissertation at Queen's University, Kingston, Ontario. In particular, I wish to thank Professors N. M. Swan and W. D. Wood, who acted as my thesis advisers and provided constructive and sympathetic guidance throughout. I am also deeply grateful to Professor D. C. Smith for his helpful comments and suggestions on the initial drafts of this study. I owe a special debt to my colleagues in the Industrial Relations Centre for their valuable support at all phases of this study. Finally, I wish to express my sincere appreciation to the Canada Department of Labour which provided financial assistance for the study through its University Research Programme.

*Pradeep Kumar**

---

* The author is Research Associate in the Industrial Relations Centre, Queen's University.

1
The Theory of Inter-Industry Wage Structure: A Review

The theory of wage structure is an attempt to explain the differentials in returns to labour services of workers of similar skill between firms, industries and regions, or in rewards to workers of varying skill. It is essential to make a distinction between the wage structure theory and the traditional wage theory: whereas wage theory relates to the determination of the price of labour, as a factor of production, wage structure theory refers to the diversity in payment to a homogeneous grade of labour and tries to explain its existence by a common phenomenon. However, to the extent that wage differentials are related to the average wage level, an inter-relationship exists between wage theory and the theory of wage structure.

Although the discussion on differential rewards for labour is an ancient pursuit, the study of wage structure as a separate entity, independent of the traditional theory of wage determination, is a recent phenomenon.[1] The emphasis on relative wage determination reflects the failure of wage theory to comprehend satisfactorily the role of trade unions in wage setting and wage regulation, and to relate the complex internal wage structure within modern organizations to wage determination in the external market.[2] While this approach has enhanced the

1 For a historical survey of wage structure theory see L. R. Salkever, *Wage Structure Theory* (New York: Humanities Press, 1964).

2 See J. T. Dunlop, ed., *The Theory of Wage Determination* (London: Macmillan, 1957), pp. 3-27. Dunlop argues that "it was not satisfactory to treat wage determination in terms of a single rate . . . the determination of wage level and the wage structure are inter-related . . . wage theory must operate with the concept of wage structure — the complex of rates within firms differentiated by occupation and employee and the complex of inter-firm rate structures . . . . Indeed, instead of reducing wage setting to the problem of a single rate, the task of analyzing wage determination is rather the problem of setting and variation in the whole structure or complex of rates." He makes a distinction between the wage structure within a plant or firm, where differentials are set by the same authority, and the complex of inter-firm structures. "One of the central problems of wage analysis," according to him, "is to indicate the inter-relationship between the internal and external wage structures." This relationship between internal and external wage structures is the main subject of a paper by G. H. Hildebrand, "External Influences and the Internal Wage Structure," in *Internal Wage Structure*, ed. J. L. Meij (Amsterdam: North-Holland, 1963), pp. 260-299.

understanding of wage setting mechanisms, it has made the development of an integrated, acceptable general theory of wages, capable of explaining wage structures and their relationship with the average wage level, more difficult. The gap between empirical research and the theoretical abstraction has become wider.[3] The search for a "realistic" explanation of wage determination has led to a division between the supporters of neo-classical price theory, who put their faith in the power of market forces of supply and demand to determine and regulate wage rates, and the institutionalists, who are convinced of the strength of unionism in influencing relative wages.[4]

More recently, however, attempts have been made to find a rough consensus between the two competing schools of thought.[5] Although these efforts have not yet produced a generally accepted theory of wages, they have helped in outlining a set of guidelines for a general theoretical framework. This chapter outlines the essence of alternative theories of wage determination which have a bearing on the study of inter-industry wage structure, and analyzes the recent modifications which may have contributed to finding a rough consensus between them.

The Competitive Theory

The neo-classical competitive theory of the labour market predicts that "in the long run, under competitive conditions, any industry will pay the same price for a given grade of labour as any other industry hiring in the same location,"[6] abstracting from the difference in non-pecuniary attri-

---

3 This gap was underlined by Reder who remarked that "most discussions of inter-industry wage differentials proceed without much explicit consideration of economic theory." See M. W. Reder, "Wage Differentials: Theory and Measurement," in *Aspects of Labour Economics*, National Bureau of Economic Research Special Conference Series No. 14 (Princeton: University Press, 1962), p. 276.

4 For a survey of current and past research, see M. W. Reder, "Wage Differentials," pp. 257-311; Daniel Mulvey, *A Study of Competing Theories of Inter-industry Wage Structure Variation* (Ph.D. thesis, Georgetown University, 1965); and *A Review of Industrial Relations Research*, Vol. 1 (Madison: Industrial Relations Research Association, 1970), pp. 79-144.

5 For a survey of recent wage theories see John Corina, *Labour Market Economics* (London: Heinemann Educational Books, 1972).

6 Reder, "Wage Differentials," pp. 276-277. Long run is defined to be a period if shifting the initial or terminal date to any other year in the same reference cycle would not alter the argument. For a mathematical formulation of the competitive model in both static and dynamic forms see F. C. Ripley, *The Structure of Wages in the United States Manufacturing Industries, 1948-1964* (Ph.D. thesis, Harvard University, 1970, published by the American Iron and Steel Institute's Committee on Educational Cooperation).

butes of industries and locations which may compensate for differences in pecuniary rewards. The competitive theory stresses equalization of net job attractiveness or net advantages for identical jobs across industries, where net advantages include both pecuniary and non-pecuniary rewards. If pecuniary rewards or monetary returns were unequal they could be compensating for differences in non-pecuniary aspects of industries. Assuming that non-pecuniary attributes of employment were the same in all industries and the price of labour to be synonymous with the wage rate, the competitive price theory maintains that observed differentials in wage rates for a similar grade of labour would be strictly temporary, arising on account of differential growth of industries and short run inelasticities of labour supply. The labour market adjusts in the long run through mobility of labour producing a tendency for equalization of wage rates.[7]

The predictions of the model are based on the following five assumptions:

There is *perfect mobility* of workers between industries. Perfect mobility is defined as the absence of non-economic barriers to mobility, i.e., partial restrictions on the demand and/or supply of labour.[8] Mobility also presupposes a perfect knowledge of the market.

There are *no economic costs*, private or social, associated with the mobility and specific to particular industries. The economic barriers to mobility are generated by private opportunity costs associated with a labour market transfer, i.e., costs of acquiring job information, costs of moving, etc.

Units of labour are homogeneous. Homogeneity implies that either the units are of the same quality and/or they are perfectly substitutable. When workers are differentiated by skills embodying training, experience etc., the earning differentials between them are approximated by the ratio of their marginal revenue productivities.

Workers and employers are rational. Workers attempt to maximize

---

7 Ripley mentions six adjustment mechanisms which describe economic behaviour in a market framework: product market competition, labour market competition, factor market competition (through substitution), international competition, technical change, and firm competition. The operation of these six adjustment mechanisms is influenced by the mode of wage setting in an industry. For example, "the forces of competition in the product market and in factor substitution are likely to be important when collective bargaining is the mode by which wages are set, because the labour market adjustment mechanism is often weakened by union control over the flow of labour into the industry." *The Structure of Wages in United States*, pp. 7-11. The effectiveness of the six adjustment mechanisms varies from industry to industry.

8 These restrictions could be in the form of closed shops, feather-bedding, non-portability of seniority and pension rights, trade licensing, apprenticeship rules, etc.

their utility functions which depict their income-leisure preferences. Employers maximize profits. The rationality assumption implies that workers prefer higher to lower incomes per unit of time. Similarly, employers prefer to pay lower rather than higher wage rates in order to minimize costs per unit of output.

Wage rates adjust so as to equate demand and supply in each market, i.e., there is *no involuntary unemployment.*[9]

Given the assumptions outlined above, the inter-industry wage differentials for workers of similar skill could only persist under competitive conditions if there were compensating differentials in non-pecuniary attributes of employment between industries. The importance of this factor was particularly emphasized by the classical economists. Adam Smith, for example, observed that

> . . . pecuniary wages are everywhere different according to different employment of labour. But this difference arises partly from certain circumstances in the employments themselves, which, either really or at least in the imagination of men, make up for a small pecuniary gain in some, and counterbalance a great one in others.[10]

He mentioned five non-pecuniary characteristics, in addition to the location of employment, that might cause differentials in wage rates: agreeableness of employment, cost of learning, security of employment, degree of trust, and probability of success. Modern economists, in their zeal for quantitative measurement, have tended to undermine the significance of non-pecuniary aspects of employment and interpreted competitive theory as predicting equalization in the price of labour (meaning

---

9 The existence of involuntary unemployment impedes the process of adjustment in that the mobility of labour is hampered on account of the lack of job opportunities or due to the downward inflexibility of money wage rates. This has led many economists to believe that the competitive model does not work in situations of less than full employment. See G. E. Johnson, "Wage Theory and Inter-regional Variations," *Industrial Relations* 6 (1967): 321-338 and A. Rees, "Wage Determination and Involuntary Unemployment," *Quarterly Journal of Economics* 59 (1951): 143-153. According to Gallaway, however, the existence of cyclical involuntary unemployment does not invalidate the competitive model if (a) cyclical unemployment is apportioned evenly throughout the system (there is a high degree of positive correlation between sectoral unemployment rates), and (b) there is no differential impact of cyclical unemployment on various sectors. L. E. Gallaway, "Labour Mobility, Resource Allocation and Structural Unemployment," *American Economic Review* 53 (1963): 694.

10 Adam Smith, *The Wealth of Nations*, 6th ed., ed. E. Canon (Strand: Methuen, 1961), Vol. 1, chap. 10, part 1.

wage rates and monetary value of employee benefits).[11] This apparent misinterpretation is the basis on which the persistence on inter-industry wage differentials for the same job in a local labour market is cited as an evidence invalidating the long run predictions of the competitive theory.[12]

The classical notion of non-pecuniary aspects of employment, as a factor in wage differentials, has been revived recently[13] partly due to the emergence of the theory of hedonistic price indexes,[14] and partly on account of the unsuccessful attempts in explaining wage differentials. It is now accepted that the influence of some of the non-pecuniary attributes, e.g., noise, temperature, safety, degree of responsibility, constancy and security of employment, can be roughly measured in quantitative terms and proxies can be used in the case of others where direct measurement may not be possible.

The competitive theory has been criticized for its heroic assumptions,[15] particularly with respect to labour mobility and full

---

11 This is reflected in Reder's survey of wage structure theory and research. After stating that the economic theory predicts equalization in the price of labour for similar work in the long run, he qualifies his remark for the differences in non-pecuniary aspects of industries. But in a footnote on the next page he maintains that "it is hard to believe — though imaginable — that industries as such, have differing degrees of non-pecuniary attractiveness to labour force members. Most of the apparent non-pecuniary differences among industries would seem to boil down to differences in the relative attractiveness of different locations and of the specific jobs offered. For example, we submit that a job as bookkeeper in the New York Office of a coal mining firm is no less attractive than a similar job in the same location in an electronics firm." See Reder, "Wage Differentials," p. 277.

12 See for example, Donald E. Cullen, "Comment," in *Aspects of Labor Economics*, pp. 311-317.

13 A. Rees, *Compensating Wage Differentials*, Working Paper No. 41 (Princeton: Industrial Relations Section, Princeton University, January 1973); S. Rosen, "On the Interindustry Wages and Hours Structure," *Journal of Political Economy* 77 (1969): 249-273, and M. A. Lutz, *The Equilibrium Wage Structure* (Ph.D. Thesis, University of California (Berkeley), 1972). According to Rees, "It would be hard to imagine a theory of relative wages that did not make use of this concept (of compensating differentials)."

14 See Robert E. B. Lucas, *Working Conditions, Wage Rates and Human Capital: A Hedonic Study* (Ph.D. Thesis, Massachussets Institute of Technology, 1972). Using the Lancasterian approach to consumer theory, where the price of commodities is related to their characteristics, Lucas fits "hedonic" wage equations to individual workers' wage rates by means of such job characteristics as aptitudes, training time, temperaments, repetitiveness of jobs, physical demands, working conditions and functional responsibilities.

15 For the significance of assumptions to the validity of the competitive theory of the labour Market see Simon Rottenberg, "On Choice in Labor Markets," *Industrial and Labor Relations Review* 9 (1956): 183-199, and a comment by Robert J. Lampman in the same Journal, pp. 629-636.

employment.[16] It is argued that there are significant barriers to mobility in modern labour markets: workers do not appear to have perfect knowledge of job opportunities and comparable wage rates, and the acquisition of knowledge is not costless as assumed by the competitive theory. There are substantial costs to workers of job search and to employers of employee search. Further, the mobility of workers is restricted because of such things as non-portability of pensions, seniority rights, licensing and apprenticeship rules and regulations. In addition to the market and institutional impediments to mobility the notion of long run static equilibrium — the point at which demand for labour is equal to the supply of labour — is considered unrealistic and a mere theoretical abstraction on the grounds that equilibrium in labour markets is only a chance occurrence. This criticism is supported by the findings of labour market research which indicate that there is always some disequilibrium in the labour market, i.e., all labour markets do not clear instantly and simultaneously. The excess demand for some occupational groups in some industries together with high employment in others is cited as an evidence of this phenomenon.[17]

The Institutional Model

The institutional wage model focuses upon labour market institutions in the analysis of differentials in wage rates for homogeneous labour across firms and industries. It emphasizes the significant role of trade unions in relative wage determination in labour markets where collective bargaining is the primary method of wage setting and industrial jurisprudence.[18] For analytical purposes the short run institutional approach can be distinguished from the long run approach to union impact on wage structure. The short run approach studies the unions' approximate influence on wage rates, examining the actual process of bargaining between labour and management. The long run approach takes account

16 See Edmund S. Phelps, *et al.*, *Microeconomic Foundations of Employment and Inflation Theory* (New York: W. W. Norton, 1970); George J. Stigler, "Information in the Labour Market," and A. Rees, "Information Networks in Labour Markets," reprinted in *Readings in Labor Market Analysis* (New York: Holt, Rinehart and Winston, 1971), pp. 231-250; and John Vanderkamp, *Mobility Behaviour in the Canadian Labour Force*, Economic Council of Canada Special Study No. 6 (Ottawa: Information Canada, 1973).

17 See Charles C. Holt, *et al.*, *The Unemployment— Inflation Dilemma: A Manpower Solution* (Washington, D.C.: The Urban Institute, 1971), pp. 46-59.

18 A. M. Ross, *Trade Union Wage Policy* (Berkeley: University of California Press, 1956), and J. T. Dunlop, *Wage Determination Under Trade Unions* (New York: Augustus M. Kelley, 1960). Also Daniel J. B. Mitchell, "Union Wage Policies: The Ross-Dunlop Controversy," *Industrial Relations* 11 (1972): 46-61. Mitchell attempts a resolution of Dunlop's "economic" union model and Ross' "political" union model by explicitly introducing the consideration of employer resistence to union wage demands.

of how unions establish permanent wage differentials through their control of labour supply and/or by enforcing employment conditions that may hinder mobility between firms and industries.

The Short Run Approach The short run institutional approach to wage determination, commonly identified by bargaining wage models,[19] emphasizes the peculiarities of each bargaining "round" where the political and financial strength of unions and management and their bargaining strategy determine "key" wage rates (and working conditions). The perception and the conceptualization of forces that influence the bargaining strategy in wage negotiations under varying market conditions provide a valuable insight into union and management wage policy-making. It enables the evaluation of market and non-market factors in short run wage determination.

Although a useful exercise in understanding wage setting and regulation, the approach has limited application to the analysis of short run inter-industry wage differentials since it is applicable only in unionized situations and to individual firms. The elements of bargaining strategy in large firms may not be representative of all firms in an industry, and the outcomes of the bargaining rounds are likely to be averaged out at the industry level, particularly in those industries where the number of firms is large and there are no multi-employer bargaining and inter-firm spill-over possibilities.

The recent research on "wage rounds", in both Canada and the United States has attempted to provide an empirical content to bargaining models.[20] The approach, however, has had very limited success for

---

19 J. Pen, *The Wage Rate Under Collective Bargaining* (Cambridge: Harvard University Press, 1959); and "A General Theory of Bargaining," *American Economic Review* 42 (1952): 24-42. Representative research on the bargaining model is also found in C. Stevens, "On the Theory of Negotiations," *Quarterly Journal of Economics* 72 (1958): 77-94; J. G. Cross, "A Theory of the Bargaining Process," *American Economic Review* (1965): 67-94; R. L. Bishop, "Game-Theoretic Analyses of Bargaining," *Quarterly Journal of Economics* 77 (1963): 559-602; J. C. Barsanyi, "Bargaining and Conflict Situations in the Light of a New Approach to Game Theory," *American Economic Review* 55 (1965): 447-457; K. W. Rothschild, "Approaches to the Theory of Bargaining," in *Theory of Wage Determination*, ed. J. T. Dunlop, pp. 281-290; B. D. Mabry, "The Pure Theory of Bargaining," *Industrial and Labor Relations Review* 18 (1965): 479-502.

20 See O. Eckstein and T. A. Wilson, "The Determination of Money Wages in American Industry," *Quarterly Journal of Economics* 76 (1962): 379-414; and G. Sparks and D. Wilton, "Determinants of Negotiated Wage Increases: An Empirical Analysis," *Econometrica* 39 (1971): 739-750, and "Wage Determination at the Industry Level" (unpublished mimeograph, 1969). The main thrust of these papers is to emphasize the discontinuity of wage adjustments in "key" industries on account of "wage bargain rounds". They start with the assumption that the bargaining process (between labour and management) is the basic determinant of wage rates under conditions of bilateral monopoly.

relative wage determination due to the problems of measuring the impact of "key-rounds" on "non-key" industries or in identifying inter-industry spill-over. The research, moreover, has concentrated on average wage increases in bargaining rounds without attempting to identify internal wage structures or the "customary" differentials in wage rates for various jobs within an organization.[21]

The Long Run Approach The long run institutional approach considers the degree of unionization as a factor in relative wage determination on the assumption that unions are able to obtain a wage premium for their members either by erecting labour mobility barriers or through holding on to short run wage gains in certain favourable labour market and product market environments, or both.[22]

A considerable volume of literature now exists on the impact of unions on relative wages and inter-industry wage structure.[23] While it is generally granted that the unions are indeed responsible for a wage premium, the size (and the statistical significance) of union non-union wage differentials is still debatable. There is also considerable disagree-

---

21 Differentials in wage rates for various jobs in an organization are presumed to depend on the technology of production, administrative work organization, union jurisdiction rules, etc. For a pioneering work on this subject see Jack Steiber, *The Steel Industry Wage Structure* (Cambridge: Harvard University Press, 1959).

22 Albert Rees, *The Economics of Trade Unions* (Chicago: University Press, 1962); John T. Dunlop, "Comment," on "The Effects of Unions on Wage Differentials," by H. G. Lewis, in *Aspects of Labor Economics*, pp. 341-344; and H. G. Lewis, "Competitive and Monopoly Unionism," and Gary S. Becker, "Union Restrictions on Entry," in *The Public Stake in Union Power*, ed. Philip D. Bradley (Charlottesville: University of Virginia Press, 1959), pp. 181-224.

23 See H. G. Lewis, *Unionism and Relative Wages in the United States: An Empirical Inquiry* (Chicago: University of Chicago Press, 1963); A. Ross, *The Economics of Trade Unions* (Chicago: University of Chicago Press, 1962); V. Fuchs, *The Service Economy* (New York: N.B.E.R., 1968), pp. 128-156; A. W. Throop, "The Union-Nonunion Wage Differential and Cost-Push Inflation," *American Economic Review* 58 (1968): 78-99; L. W. Weiss, "Concentration and Labor Earnings," *American Economic Review* 56 (1966): 96-117; H. M. Levinson, "Unionism, Concentration and Wage Changes: Towards a Unified Theory," *Industrial and Labor Relations Review* 20 (1967): 198-205; a collection of articles under the general heading "Effects of the Union: A Symposium," *Industrial and Labor Relations Review* 24 (1971): 159-202; W. R. Bailey and others, "Wage Differentials and Establishment Size, Union Status and Industry Concentration," *American Statistical Association Proceedings*, 1970, pp. 395-401; Orley Ashenfelter and George E. Johnson, "Unionism, Relative Wages and Labour Quality in U.S. Manufacturing Industries," *International Economic Review* 13 (1972): 488-508; S. Rosen, "Unionism and the Occupational Wage Structure in the United States," *International Economic Review* 11 (1970): 269-286; and S. R. Reber, *The Effects of Unionism upon Relative Wages* (Ph.D. Thesis, University of Chicago, 1970).

ment about the independent role of unions in establishing wage differentials. The findings of empirical research into union effects on relative wage rates can be summarized as follows:

First, union influence on relative wages does not seem to be independent of the product market environment. Most studies have found a very high correlation between the degree of unionization, wage rates and the industry concentration ratio, a proxy for the degree of monopoly in the product market.

Secondly, the nature and mechanism of institutional influence on the operation of labour markets is still vague. It is not yet clear if the unions have once and for all influence on relative wage rates and/or whether they affect the wage adjustment mechanism. The institutional wage adjustment model suggests that although wage changes are determined by excess demand in the labour market, the size of adjustment is dependent on the degree of unionization and the degree of monopoly in the product market.[24]

Thirdly, There is considerable debate on the significance of institutional influence on wage determination under varying conditions of aggregate demand. Some economists have argued that the unions have their greatest impact on relative wages in a less than full employment environment. Others maintain that unions are most effective in full employment situations, especially at the peak of the business cycle when the demand for labour is strong.

Finally, the union's relative wage effects are related to the skill-mix of industries. There are many dimensions of this relationship. First, high wage industries are generally those that employ a high proportion of skilled labour: because the hiring and training of skilled workers require a greater investment per man than for unskilled workers, employers of

---

24 For the union role in wage adjustment see A. G. Hines, "Trade Unions and Wage Inflation in the United Kingdom, 1893-1961," *The Review of Economic Studies* 31 (1964): 221-282; J. Vanderkamp, "Wage and Price Level Determination: An Empirical Model for Canada," *Economica* 33 (1966): 194-218; Robert Swidinsky, "Trade Unions and the Rate of Change of Money Wages in Canada, 1953-70," *Industrial and Labor Relations Review* 25 (1972): 363-375; M. L. Wachter, "Relative Wage Equations for U.S. Manufacturing Industries," *Review Of Economics and Statistics* 52 (1970): 405-410. S. A. Behman, "Wage Changes, Institutions, and Relative Factor Prices in Manufacturing," *Review of Economics and Statistics* 51 (1969): 227-238. While Hines-Swidinsky correlate union activity and wage changes, Wachter derives the realtionship between industry's relative wage response to the unemployment rate and the degree of unionization. Sara Behman, on the other hand, treats institutional variables as shift variables in the wage equation. For a reconciliation of these approaches see O. C. Ashenfelter, G. E. Johnson and J. N. Penceval, "Trade Unions and the Rate of Change of Money Wages in the United States Manufacturing Industry," *Review of Economic Studies* 39 (1972): 27-54.

skilled workers pay a higher wage to skilled workers, independently of unionization, to keep labour turnover low. The estimate of union non-union wage differentials may, therefore, be biased upwards in the high skill-mix industries.[25] Secondly, unions may affect the skill-mix of industries by limiting labour quality adjustments, particularly in tight labour markets.[26] The union's ability to limit skill substitution may be an important factor in relative wage differentials.[27] Thirdly, industrial unions aim at maintaining intra-plant equities in occupational wage relationships. This union wage policy is reflected in a lower percentage spread in the wage rates for skilled and unskilled workers in the unionized industries.[28]

The inter-relationship between the degree of unionization, skill-mix, internal wage differentials and relative wage rates suggests that the independent relative wage impact of unions may be asymmetric across occupational groups. Unions may have more influence in creating a wage differential for unskilled workers than for skilled workers.

Recent Wage Models

The Skilled Worker Hypothesis The skilled worker hypothesis[29] postulates that while wage rates for skilled labour are determined by com-

25 Throop, "Union-Nonunion Wage Differential".

26 M. W. Reder, "Wage Structure and Structural Unemployment," *Review of Economic Studies* 31 (1964): 309-322, and Ashenfelter and Johnson, "Unionism, Relative Wages and Labour Quality".

27 See Sidney R. Finkel and Vincent J. Tarasus, "A Theoretical Integration of Production and Wage Theory," *Western Economic Journal* 7 (1969): 371-378.

28 Robert L. Raimon, "The Indeterminateness of Wages of Semi-skilled Workers," *Industrial and Labor Relations Review* 6 (1953): 180-194; Hildebrand, "External Influences", and Pradeep Kumar, "Differentials in Wage Rates of Unskilled Labour in the Canadian Manufacturing Industries," *Industrial and Labor Relations Review* 26 (1972): 631-645.

29 S. A. Behman, *Wage Determination in a Cyclical Setting* (Ph.D. Thesis, University of California (Berkeley), 1966), "Wage Determination Process in U.S. Manufacturing," *Quarterly Journal of Economics* 76 (1968): 117-142, and "Labour Mobility, Increasing Labour Demand and Money Wage Rate Increases in United States Manufacturing," *Review of Economic Studies* 31 (1964): 253-266; J. R. Hicks, "Economic Foundations of Wage Policy," *Economic Journal* 65 (1955): 389-404. For the purpose of this hypothesis skilled workers are those: (1) who have learned their trade through apprenticeship or have acquired their skill by informal on-the-job training, and (2) whose skills are transferable among industries. Excluded are the workers who have reached the skill level through upgrading and training within a firm or industry. Such workers have an employer or an industry orientation rather than market orientation. In other words the hypothesis applies only to workers with "general training" and not with "specific training".

petitive market forces of supply and demand, wages for unskilled and semi-skilled workers are governed by institutional forces. The relevance of the competitive theory to skilled workers is emphasized on the grounds that skilled workers are the most mobile group of the labour force, they respond to marginal adjustments in wage rates as postulated by traditional economic theory,[30] they have virtually no involuntary unemployment, and even in conditions of deficient aggregate demand do not face the prospect of lay-offs because of the high cost of selecting and training skills. Moreover, in most production processes, while it is easier to substitute skilled for unskilled labour, it is not feasible to substitute unskilled for skilled workers.[31] The conclusion is supported by many labour market studies which have found that skilled workers appear to have better information about wages, working conditions and available jobs in their trades than the unskilled and semi-skilled workers.[32] The low rate of lay-off and of voluntary quit among skilled workers and in industries employing a high proportion of skilled labour are also cited in support of the hypothesis.

The skilled worker hypothesis is very similar to the general theory of occupational wage differentials outlined by Reder.[33] The theory postulates that while the wage rates of skilled labour are determined by

---

30 D. E. Leigh, "An Empirical Investigation of the Determinants of the Level of Unemployment in Six Major Occupations," *Western Economic Journal* 10 (1972): 384-395. Leigh, using 1958-1970 seasonally adjusted monthly data, found relatively large and statistically significant short run real wage elasticities for skilled craftsmen and foremen. He concluded that skilled workers respond to change in their real wages.

31 See Reder, "Wage Structure", and W. Y. Oi, "Labor as a Quasi-fixed Factor of Production," *Journal of Political Economy* 70 (1962): 538-555. While the argument appears reasonable in theory, it has been found difficult to verify it empirically, primarily because of the poor quality of the data on occupational wages and employment. The limited empirical research does indicate a very low elasticity of substitution between skilled and unskilled workers. See T. M. Power, *Elasticities of Substitution Between Different Types of Labour: Theoretical Analysis and Empirical Examples* (Ph.D. Thesis, Princeton University, 1972); and M. S. Cohen, *The Determinants of the Relative Supply and Demand for Unskilled Workers* (Ph.D. Thesis, M.I.T., 1967).

32 G. P. Schultz, *Recent Research on Labor Mobility*, Series 2, No. 34 (Cambridge: M.I.T., December, 1951); L. G. Reynolds, *Structure of Labor Markets*, Bulletin No. 65 (New York: Social Science Research Council, 1954). The smaller dispersion in wage rates for skilled labour compared to unskilled and semi-skilled labour is considered to be a consequence of this mobility behaviour (see Johnson, "Wage Theory and Inter-regional Variations," pp. 327-338, and Raimon, "Indeterminateness of Wages," pp. 181-194). Johnson's calculations reveal a narrowing trend in wage differentials for skilled workers during 1952-1965.

33 M. W. Reder, "Theory of Occupational Wage Differentials," *American Economic Review* 65 (1955): 833-852, and "Wage Structure and Structural Unemployment," pp. 312-315.

the market forces of supply and demand, the unskilled wage rates are set by some notion of a "social minimum". Reder's social minimum for unskilled labour is an intellectual construct (not directly observable) determined by "extra-economic" forces, presumably by statute in the form of minimum wage or through trade union wage policy (the policy of equitable wage increase for all occupational groups), or both. Reder argues that the hourly compensation for unskilled labour is not a flexible market price. The wage rate for the unskilled adjusts with great sluggishness, if at all, to the presence of unemployment.

The "skilled worker" hypothesis and the theory of occupational wage differentials attempt to explain the relationship between skill margins (the percentage differential between occupational wage rates within an industry) and the differentials in wage rates between industries for skilled and unskilled occupations. They provide a ground work for integrating the competitive market theory with the institutional wage model by suggesting the possibility of institutional barriers to mobility and factor substitution, and by considering the significance of trade union wage policy in non-market determination of wage rates for unskilled labour.

The Spill-Over Hypothesis A variant of the institutional model, the spill-over hypothesis maintains that there are in fact two types of labour markets: one, where wage levels and wage increases are nearly similar because of the common product market and institutional links, and the other, where wage rates are determined purely by market forces. While the two markets are independent there is some spill-over from the predominantly institutional labour market to the competitive market.[34]

The implication of this hypothesis is that both the institutional and market factors are important in relative wage determination. The hypo-

34 Eckstein and Wilson, "Determination of Money Wages"; J. E. Maher, "The Wage Pattern in the United States, 1946-1957," *Industrial and Labor Relations Review* 15 (1961): 3-20; Rees, *Economics of Trade Unions*; J. T. Dunlop, "The Task of Contemporary Wage Theory," in *New Concepts in Wage Determination*, ed. G. W. Taylor and F. C. Pierson (Toronto: McGraw-Hill, 1957); T. W. McGuire and L. A. Rapping, "Inter-industry Wage Change Dispersion and the 'Spillover' Hypothesis," *American Economic Review* 56 (1966): 493-501, and "The Role of Market Variables and Key Bargains in the Manufacturing Wage Determination Process," *Journal of Political Economy* 76 (1968): 1015-1036; D. S. Hamermesh, *Interdependence in the Labor Market*, Working Paper No. 32 (Princeton: Industrial Relation Section, Princeton University, 1971). For a dynamic market interdependence model see F. Brechling, "Wage Inflation and the Structure of Regional Unemployment," *Journal of Money, Credit and Banking* 5, Part II (1973): 355-384. Although the model is tested for regional differentials in wage changes, it could be easily extended to inter-industry and inter-occupational variations. Brechling's model outlines spillover effects through expectations from "tight" sectors to "looser" ones.

thesis does not predict either the size of relative wage dispersion at a moment of time or the trend over time in wage differentials.[35] It simply outlines the inter-dependence of the two apparently segmented labour markets. The terminology used to describe this process varies considerably, i.e., spill-over, key bargains, wage leadership, pattern wage adjustment, orbits of coercive comparisons, demonstration effect, wage contours and wage diffusion.

The main problem in the test of the "spill-over" variable is the difficulty in isolating the institutional influence from the labour supply effects.[36] Moreover it is not clear whether spill-over is from the highly organized and oligopolistic market to the non-unionized competitive sector or from the competitive sector to the unionized sector. In the case of Canada, the spill-over may not be purely domestic. Since a large percentage of the product market is controlled by American industry, wage leadership may come from across the border.[37] This will certainly be true of industries like automobile manufacturing, where unions negotiate nearly similar wage agreements, and firms produce for both Canadian and American markets.

The Manpower Flow Model The competitive model of the labour market is cast in terms of static constructs of supply and demand schedules. The manpower flow model emphasizes the dynamic character of labour markets in which there is a continuous inflow and outflow of workers.[38]

---

35 See McGuire and Rapping, "Interindustry Wage Change Dispersion", p. 495.

36 T. W. McGuire and L. A. Rapping, "The Determination of Money Wages in American Industry: Comment," *Quarterly Journal of Economics* 75 (1967): 684-690.

37 G. L. Reuber, "Wage Adjustments in Canadian Industry, 1953-1966," *Review of Economic Studies* 37 (1970): 449-468; Sparks and Wilton, "Negotiated Wage Increases"; C. H. Anderson, "Wage Spill-over Mechanisms: A U.S.-Canadian Analysis," *Industrial Relations* 11 (1972): 172-182; John Crispo, *International Unionism* (Toronto: McGraw-Hill, 1967); and B. M. Downie, *Relationship Between Canadian-American Wage Settlements* (Kingston, Ontario: Industrial Relations Centre, Queen's University, 1970). In general most Canadian studies on industrial wage determination use comparable U.S. industry wage rates as one of the exogeneous variables in their wage equations.

38 C. C. Holt, "Job Search, Phillips' Wage Relation, and Union Influence: Theory and Evidence," in *Microeconomic Foundations of Employment and Inflation Theory*, by Edmund S. Phelps *et al.* (New York: W. W. Norton, 1970), pp. 53-123; Holt, *Unemployment-Inflation Dilemma*; and Holt, "Concepts of Job Vacancies in a Dynamic Theory of the Labour Market," in *The Measurement and Interpretation of Job Vacancies* (New York: National Bureau of Economic Research, 1966), pp. 73-141. The model has been inspired by the dynamics of frictional unemployment. See M. W. Reder, "The Theory of Frictional Unemployment," *Economica* 36 (1969): 1-29 and G. E. Johnson, *Non-Linearities in the Labour Market Adjustment Process*, Working Paper No. 3 (Princeton: Industrial Relations Section, Princeton University, 1967).

"Workers flow into the market as they leave the family, graduate from schools, quit previous employment, and are laid off, and they leave the market as new hires, recalls, or they return to family or school. This high flow through the market keeps it in a constant state of flux and makes it respond quickly to changing economic conditions."[39] The dynamic interaction between the stocks of unemployed workers and job vacancies and the relationships that govern the flow into and out of these stocks provide the setting for wage determination and wage adjustment. According to this model the inter-industry wage differentials for a similar grade of labour depend on the probabilities per period of time of finding jobs and employees and the probability distributions of the durations of unemployment, vacancies and jobs. The model suggests that the wage differentials among industries decline when unemployment is low and vacancies are high, and widen under conditions of high unemployment and low vacancies.

Although the "manpower flow" model does not differ significantly from the competitive model in its implications, it provides a dynamic view of the labour market. The main problem with the model is that it is difficult to estimate the complex behavioural relationships on which it is based, i.e., probabilities of job search behaviour.

A Rough Consensus

The various modifications to the competitive model and the recent empirical tests of the market and institutional factors affecting the inter-industry wage differentials provide a rough "consensus" on the basic elements of an integrated theory of relative wage determination. Some of the salient features of this consensus can be outlined as follows:

The competitive theory of the labour market, in which the forces of supply and demand for labour determine the price of labour, is the basic framework for the study of relative wage determination. Because of its logical consistency and strong links with price theory, it provides a testable model capable of modifications to take account of the dynamic aspects of the labour market, of the institutional influence on wage determination, as well as of the interaction effects of the institutional and market factors.

In using the competitive labour market model, the compensating effects of non-pecuniary attributes of industries on wage differentials need to be clearly outlined. It is possible to devise quantitative meas-

---

39 Holt, "Job Search", p. 56.

urements of non-pecuniary factors either directly or through proxy variables.

In contemporary labour markets, where collective bargaining between organized labour and management is a major instrument of wage setting and industrial jurisprudence, the role of trade unions in creating wage differentials for workers of similar skill should be recognized. However, since unions influence both wage rates and working conditions, and because it may be easier to organize workers in large firms than in small firms, the relative wage effects of unionization may not be independent of market factors and the structure of the product market.

The theory of wage differential should consider the dynamic characteristics of the labour market. First, bacause of a continuous inflow and outflow of workers in the labour market, it may be difficult to distinguish between short run and long run effects of factors affecting the demand for and the supply of labour. Secondly, if there are sharp differences in occupational labour markets, as the authors of the skilled workers hypothesis maintain, it may not be possible to gauge the independent effects of market and institutional factors on the relative wage determination for particular occupational groups. For example, it is argued that the skilled labour market is competitive, but it is not so with unskilled and semi-skilled occupational labour markets. Because of this uneven character of labour markets, trade unions may be able to transmit wage increases for skilled workers, caused by excess demand in the skilled labour market, to unskilled workers who may be in relative excess supply. As a consequence, wage inflation in one labour market may yield higher money wages in all labour markets.

Finally, the theory of inter-industry wage structure should take account of the inter-dependence of labour markets. This inter-dependence may be related to the technology of production or the growth of industrial unions, and is manifested in the inter-relationship in occupational wage rates as well as in the strong links existing between the internal wage structure within an industry and the external wage structure for similar grades of labour between industries.

In brief, the consensus outlines that the explanations for the inter-industry wage differentials for workers of similar skill include both the market and institutional factors, and that these differentials are interrelated with the structure of occupational wage rates within industries.

2

An Analysis of Wage Differentials in Canadian Industries

This chapter examines the differentials in wage rates of unskilled labourers and maintenance mechanics in 26 Canadian manufacturing industries. The purpose of the analysis is to investigate the relative magnitude and the inter-temporal behaviour of inter-industry wage differentials for workers of similar skill. Since unskilled workers and maintenance mechanics constitute only 15 per cent of the total manufacturing employment, wage rates of the two occupations are correlated with each other and with average hourly earnings to determine if some industries pay higher wages than others to all workers, irrespective of their skill level, or only to workers of particular skills.

A major part of the chapter is devoted to the differentials in wage rates of unskilled labourers for whom consistent wage data are available since 1952. The analysis of differentials in wage rates of maintenance mechanics covers the recent period, 1961-1970.

The first section analyzes the stability of and changes in wage rates for unskilled labour during the period 1952-1970; the stability of the wage structure is measured by the coefficient of product-moment correlation between industry wage levels in two terminal years. The effect of wage changes on the inter-temporal behaviour of wage differentials is investigated by correlating wage levels in the base year, 1952, with the cents-per-hour and percentage wage changes during 1952-1970. The next section studies the absolute and relative dispersion in wage rates of unskilled labourers. The third section examines the differentials in wage rates of skilled maintenance mechanics. It also explores if some industries pay better than others to all their workers, irrespective of their skill level. This hypothesis is tested by examining the differentials in average hourly earnings in the sample of 26 industries and comparing these differentials with the differentials in wage rates of unskilled labourers and maintenance mechanics. The fourth section examines the relationship between wage rates and wage supplements, from the available data, to investigate whether differentials in wage rates can be generalized for the differentials in total compensation. The results of the analysis, together with their implications, are summarized in the final section.

Wage Data The wage rates used in this study are straight time average hourly rates, which exclude the monetary value of employee benefits, overtime payments and shift differentials. They are based on a survey of establishment wage rates within industries.[1] Industry averages for a given occupation are derived by multiplying wage rates in each establishment by the number of workers receiving each rate, and then dividing the sum of the product by the total number of employees in the occupation in a given industry. In the opinion of some analysts the industry wage data is subject to serious problems because the wage variations among establishments within a given industry far exceed variations in wage rates between industries. In spite of this problem we use industry data because of the significant theoretical and policy implications of inter-industry wage differentials. A further discussion of this problem will be found in Appendix C.

The sample of 26 industries, whose wage rates are analyzed, are classified according to the *Standard Industrial Classification Manual*[2] and include an equal number of durable and non-durable manufacturing industries. They account for nearly two-thirds of the total employment of unskilled labourers and maintenance mechanics in all manufacturing industries.

Structure of Wage Rates for Unskilled Labour: Stability and Change

Table 1 shows the hierarchy of wage rates for unskilled labour in 26 manufacturing industries in 1952 and 1970. It reveals that significant disparities exist in wage rates for unskilled workers, and have been persistent over nearly two decades since 1952. For example, unskilled labour wage rates ranged from 68 cents an hour in the furniture industry to $1.48 an hour in the motor vehicle manufacturing industry in 1952. In 1970, although the cents-per-hour difference in hourly wages in the two

---

1 See Canada Department of Labour, *Wage Rates, Salaries and Hours of Labour* (Ottawa: Information Canada, annual).

2 See the *Standard Industrial Classification Manual* (Ottawa: Dominion Bureau of Statistics, 1960). The names and the S.I.C. code numbers of industries are given in Appendix A. There were some changes made in the classification of industries in 1966. The change, however, did not affect the coverage of industries included in this study. For a detailed description of these changes see Canada Department of Labour, *Wage Rates, Salaries and Hours of Labour, 1966,* Report No. 49, pp. 11-12.

Table 1

Inter-Indusrty Structure of Wage Rates for Unskilled Labour 1952-1970

Industry	Hourly wage rates in $		Relative wage rates*	
	1952	1970	1952	1970
Furniture	0.68	2.06	59	74
Bakeries	0.89	2.76	77	99
Biscuits	0.92	2.44	79	88
Paper boxes & bags	0.98	2.47	84	89
Dairy factories	1.00	2.31	86	83
Leather tanneries	1.01	2.54	87	91
Pharmaceuticals	1.02	2.48	88	89
Rubber products	1.03	2.61	89	94
Office & store machinery	1.08	2.44	93	88
Machine shops	1.09	2.30	94	83
Aircraft & parts	1.14	2.88	98	104
Veneer mills	1.15	2.55	99	92
Agricultural implements	1.22	2.69	105	97
Metal stamping, etc.	1.26	2.57	109	92
Small electric appliances	1.26	2.67	109	96
Industrial electric equipment	1.26	2.69	109	97
Breweries	1.27	3.75	109	135
Tobacco products	1.27	3.46	109	124
Iron foundries	1.27	2.85	109	102
Pulp and paper	1.27	3.12	109	112
Meat packing	1.28	3.06	110	110
Industrial chemicals	1.31	3.07	113	110
Petroleum refineries	1.35	3.22	116	116
Motor vehicle parts	1.36	3.09	117	111
Iron and steel mills	1.41	3.00	122	108
Motor vehicles assembly	1.48	3.24	128	116
Unweighted average	1.16	2.78	100	100

* Relative rates are the ratio of each industry's wage rate and the unweighted average wage, multiplied by 100.

industries was smaller than in 1952, their relative position in the inter-industry wage structure was almost unchanged: the wage rates of unskilled labour were still the lowest in the furniture industry and one of the highest in the motor vehicles industry. This stability in the relative wage position of industries is further confirmed by the coefficients of correlation in hourly wage rates in 26 industries between 1952 and the following years:

Years Correlated	*Coefficients*
1952 and 1957	0.895*
1952 and 1962	0.836*
1952 and 1970	0.738*
1957 and 1962	0.928*
1957 and 1970	0.889*
1962 and 1970	0.915*

* Statistically significant at the .001 probability level.

The positive and high correlation coefficients indicate that the inter-industry hierarchy of wage rates was stable over time (a detailed matrix of coefficients of correlation in wage rates of unskilled labourers is given in Table 2). The stability in inter-industry wage structure implies that if an industry in 1952 was paying higher wage rates to unskilled workers than other industries, the wage rates in that industry in 1970 were still above average.[3] In other words, the relative wage position of industries was almost unchanged in the two decades since 1952.

The relative wage rates of unskilled workers in Table 1, and the coefficients of correlation in industry wage levels between 1952 and the following years, indicate that although the relative wage position of industries was almost unchanged, it was not exactly the same in 1952 and 1970; there were some shifts in relative wage position of certain industries, but these shifts were few and too weak to make any noticeable impact on the overall inter-industry wage structure. Table 1 shows that

3 An Ordinary Least Squares regression on wage rates of unskilled labourers in 1968-70 revealed that nearly two-thirds of the variations in hourly wage rates in the sample of 26 industries were associated with the structure of wage rates in base years, 1952-54 (the wage rates were averaged over three years to eliminate year-to-year fluctuations). The estimated relationship was as follows:

$$Y = \underset{(2.04)^*}{0.58} + \underset{(7.10)^*}{1.63X} \qquad \bar{R}^2 = 0.664$$

where X and Y are wage levels in 1952-54 and 1968-70 respectively, figures in parenthesis are student t-values, and * means the coefficients are statistically significant at the .05 probability level.

Table 2

Correlation Matrix of Unskilled Labour Wage Rates in 26 Manufacturing Industries, 1952-1970

(In Pairs of Years)

	1952	1953	1954	1955	1956	1957	1958	1959	1960	1961	1962	1963	1964	1965	1966	1967	1968	1969
1953	0.95																	
1954	0.95	0.98																
1955	0.94	0.95	0.95															
1956	0.90	0.93	0.92	0.97														
1957	0.90	0.94	0.92	0.96	0.98													
1958	0.87	0.92	0.90	0.94	0.96	0.98												
1959	0.85	0.89	0.90	0.88	0.90	0.91	0.94											
1960	0.80	0.86	0.86	0.87	0.90	0.92	0.95	0.97										
1961	0.79	0.86	0.86	0.87	0.90	0.92	0.95	0.95	0.98									
1962	0.84	0.88	0.88	0.91	0.93	0.93	0.96	0.95	0.97	0.98								
1963	0.83	0.89	0.89	0.92	0.92	0.93	0.96	0.93	0.94	0.96	0.97							
1964	0.83	0.89	0.87	0.92	0.92	0.93	0.95	0.88	0.91	0.94	0.96	0.98						
1965	0.79	0.86	0.85	0.90	0.90	0.90	0.93	0.87	0.91	0.93	0.96	0.98	0.99					
1966	0.80	0.87	0.84	0.91	0.91	0.90	0.92	0.81	0.83	0.84	0.88	0.93	0.94	0.93				
1967	0.79	0.85	0.81	0.89	0.89	0.91	0.92	0.83	0.85	0.86	0.89	0.93	0.94	0.92	0.96			
1968	0.80	0.87	0.85	0.91	0.90	0.90	0.92	0.82	0.84	0.86	0.90	0.94	0.95	0.94	0.96	0.97		
1969	0.72	0.80	0.77	0.86	0.86	0.87	0.90	0.78	0.82	0.84	0.88	0.92	0.95	0.94	0.95	0.96	0.97	
1970	0.74	0.82	0.79	0.86	0.87	0.89	0.92	0.84	0.87	0.90	0.91	0.95	0.95	0.94	0.89	0.91	0.91	0.94

Ship To:

AMZ ORDERS APTP
800 AVONDALE AVE
COLUMBUS, OH 43212-3473

Order ID: 114-9112265-8283407

Thank you for buying from gfernald on Amazon Marketplace.

Shipping Address:	Order Date:	Thu, Sep 24, 2026
AMZ ORDERS APTP	Shipping Service:	Standard
800 AVONDALE AVE	Buyer Name:	John
COLUMBUS, OH 43212-3473	Seller Name:	gfernald

Quantity	Product Details
1	**Relative wage differentials in Canadian industries (Research and current issues series ; no. 25) [Hardcover] [1974] Kumar, Pradeep** **SKU:** GR-O9TM-2QDP **ASIN:** 0888860609 **Condition:** Used - Very Good **Order Item ID:** 170715967565921

... front endpaper was cut off, rest of inside is excellent.

Returning your item:

Go to "Your Account" on Amazon.com, click "Your Orders" and then click the "seller profile" link for this order to get information about the return and refund policies that apply.

Visit https://www.amazon.com/returns to print a return shipping label. Please have your order ID ready.

Thanks for buying on Amazon Marketplace. To provide feedback for the seller please visit www.amazon.com/feedback. To contact the seller, go to Your Orders in Your Account. Click the seller's name under the appropriate product. Then, in the "Further Information" section, click "Contact the Seller."

in 10 of the 26 industries relative wage rates changed by more than 10 per cent between 1952 and 1970. These industries were in both the lower and upper extremes of the inter-industry wage hierarchy. The relative wage gains were most prominent in breweries, tobacco products, furniture and dairy industries. On the other hand, the relative wage position of iron and steel mills, motor vehicles, machine shops, metal stamping and coating, small electric appliances, and electric industrial equipment declined during 1952-1970. These changes, however, were not very dramatic; not one of the industries in the top or the bottom of the wage hierarchy switched places. The significance of these changes to the inter-temporal behaviour of the wage structure can be examined by studying the relationship between wage levels in 1952-54 and the cents-per-hour and percentage wage changes during the period 1952-54 to 1968-70.

Relationship Between Wage Levels and Wage Changes The correlation between wage levels in 1952-54 (wage levels were averaged over three years to eliminate year-to-year fluctuations) and wage changes from 1952-54 to 1968-70 indicated that wage gains (in cents-per-hour) were partly across-the-board and partly related to the base year wage rates. An across-the-board or a flat rate cents-per-hour wage change in all industries is manifested in a statistically significant inverse relationship between wage levels and percentage wage changes (the coefficient of correlation for 26 industries was -0.45, significant at the .05 probability level). The relationship suggests that because of flat rate increases, wage gains were higher in industries paying a below average wage in 1952-54 than those industries where unskilled workers were receiving above average wage rates. If all the wage increases during 1952-54 to 1968-70 were flat rate, the inter-industry wage differentials would have compressed. This, however, was not the case. It appears that part of the wage increase was also related to the base year wage rates. This was suggested by the positive correlation between 1952-54 wage levels and the cents-per-hour wage increase in 26 industries (the coefficient of correlation was 0.49, statistically significant at the .01 probability level). The relationship implies that wage increases, in cents-per-hour, were higher in those industries where wage rates were already very high. The inter-industry wage structure may have been stable because of these two offsetting wage improvements; the flat rate wage increase leads to a narrowing of the wage differentials, while the base year related increase tends to widen the differentials.

These two counteracting effects on the inter-industry wage differentials (across-the-board increase and initial wage level-related increase) can be separated, in an approximate manner, by fitting a linear equation of the form Y = a+bX, where Y represents cents-per-hour wage increases and X stands for original level of earnings in 26 industries. The parameter *a* in this equation indicates the strength of the across-the-board increases. The parameter *b* provides the size of the wage increases related to the base year wage levels. The test yielded the following estimate of the equation:

$$Y = \underset{(2.04)^*}{0.576} + \underset{(2.74)^*}{0.628X}$$

The equation reveals that of the average $1.34 wage increase in 26 industries between 1952-54 to 1968-70, 58 cents was in the form of a flat rate increase and the remaining 76 cents increase was related to the base year wage level (amounting to a 63 per cent increase). The base year related wage gains ranged from $0.39 or 34 per cent of the total wage in office and store machinery to $1.42 or 101 per cent in breweries. Table 3 shows that the base year related gains in 10 of the 26 industries were closer (in 5 per cent range) to the average increase of 63 per cent, below the average increase in 8 industries and above the average in another 8 industries. In industries where the base year related wage increases were higher than the average increase for all industries, relative wage rates for unskilled workers showed significant improvement. These industries included breweries, bakeries, biscuits, and tobacco products. Conversely, relative wage rates of unskilled workers declined in industries like iron and steel mills, iron foundries, industrial electric equipment, small electric appliances, metal stamping and coating, machine shops and office and store machinery, where base year related wage gains were below the all industry average. Relative wage position of unskilled workers in industries in which base year related wage improvements were close to the average of 26 industries was unaffected.

Dispersion in Wage Rates for Unskilled Labour

Table 4 gives various measures of dispersion in wage rates for unskilled labour in 26 Canadian manufacturing industries. Absolute dispersion in cents-per-hour is measured by the inter-quartile range, standard deviation and the difference in mean wage rates of the eight highest and the eight lowest paying industries of 1952. The coefficient of variation, the coefficient of dispersion, and the percentage difference in mean wage

Table 3

Industry Wage Levels and Wage Changes, 1952-1970

	Wage levels ($)		Wage changes ($)		
Industry	1952-54	1968-70	Total change	Flat rate change*	Base year related change
Furniture	0.81	1.83	1.02	0.58	0.44
Bakeries	0.94	2.40	1.46	0.58	0.86
Biscuits	0.97	2.35	1.38	0.58	0.80
Paper boxes & bags	1.04	2.31	1.27	0.58	0.69
Dairy factories	1.04	2.26	1.22	0.58	0.64
Leather tanneries	1.06	2.29	1.23	0.58	0.65
Pharmaceuticals	1.04	2.27	1.23	0.58	0.65
Rubber products	1.11	2.41	1.30	0.58	0.72
Office & store machinery	1.14	2.11	0.97	0.58	0.39
Machine shops	1.15	2.15	1.00	0.58	0.42
Aircraft & parts	1.23	2.68	1.45	0.58	0.87
Veneer mills	1.13	2.44	1.31	0.58	0.73
Agricultural implements	1.30	2.66	1.36	0.58	0.78
Metal stamping, etc.	1.33	2.49	1.16	0.58	0.58
Small electric appliances	1.24	2.37	1.13	0.58	0.55
Industrial electric equipment	1.30	2.42	1.12	0.58	0.54
Breweries	1.40	1.40	2.00	0.58	1.42
Tobacco products	1.37	3.08	1.71	0.58	1.13
Iron foundries	1.31	2.53	1.22	0.58	0.64
Pulp & paper	1.35	2.90	1.55	0.58	0.97
Meat packing	1.33	2.80	1.47	0.58	0.89
Industrial chemicals	1.33	2.87	1.54	0.58	0.96
Petroleum refineries	1.41	2.98	1.57	0.58	0.99
Motor vehicle parts	1.42	2.86	1.43	0.58	0.85
Iron & steel mills	1.45	2.71	1.26	0.58	0.68
Motor vehicles assembly	1.52	3.06	1.54	0.58	0.96
Unweighted average	1.22	2.56	1.34	0.58	0.76

* The flat rate and the base year related wage changes are calculated from the estimate of the least square regression, $Y = 0.58 + 0.63X$ where Y is total cents per hour wage change during 1952-54 to 1968-70 and X is industry levels of wage rates in 1952-54.

rates of the eight highest and the eight lowest paying industries provide estimates of the relative wage differentials.[4]

Table 4

Dispersion in Wage Rates of Unskilled Labour in 26 Manufacturing Industries, 1952-1970

Year	Inter-quartile range (in cents)	Coeffifient of disper-sion (in percentage terms)	Standard deviation (in cents)	Coefficient of variation (in percen-tage terms)	Differences in mean wage rate of high-low industries of 1952*	
					Absolute (in cents)	Per cent
1952	25	20.16	18	15.8	40	43
1953	26	20.63	19	15.4	40	40
1954	33	24.81	18	14.0	38	36
1955	34	25.47	18	14.2	39	36
1956	31	22.88	20	14.6	42	36
1957	36	25.62	23	15.7	47	39
1958	38	26.29	23	15.1	45	35
1959	37	24.42	23	15.0	46	35
1960	38	23.82	25	15.4	46	33
1961	44	26.43	27	16.2	48	34
1962	49	28.99	27	15.7	51	35
1963	44	25.88	28	15.6	49	32
1964	44	25.14	29	15.7	51	33
1965	47	25.98	30	15.8	52	32
1966	52	25.87	32	15.8	55	31
1967	47	22.65	33	15.3	55	29
1968	52	23.16	34	14.5	58	28
1969	52	20.84	36	14.2	53	23
1970	59	21.93	39	14.1	62	25

* Refers to unweighted average of wage rates in 8 highest paying and 8 lowest paying industries.

4 The various measures differ in their coverage. The inter-quartile range and the coefficient of dispersion around the median wage rate are based on the three quartiles of wage distribution. The differences in wage rates of the highest and lowest paying industries cover wage rates in industries on the two extremes of the wage hierarchy. The standard deviation and the coefficient of variation cover the whole wage distribution.

The standard deviation and the coefficient of variation are generally considered the best and the most reliable indicators of absolute and relative wage differentials respectively because they cover the complete wage distribution. The other measures are limited in their coverage but useful in providing information about certain important aspects of wage structure. For example, the competitive theory maintains that wage rates in some industries may be unusually high at a point in time on account of short-run rigidities in the labour market, but they tend to equalize over time partly because of the expanded supply of labour in the long run and partly due to the factor substitution.[5] This argument can be verified by examining the percentage differentials in mean wage rates of industries on the upper and lower extremes of the wage hierarchy. Similarly the coefficient of dispersion, based on the ratio of interquartile range and median, provides additional insight into the differentials in wage rates in industries on the three quartiles of the wage distribution.

The table reveals that although the absolute dispersion in wage rates for unskilled labour across 26 Canadian manufacturing industries more than doubled during 1952-1970, the relative wage dispersion did not change significantly: the coefficient of dispersion (around the median of wage rates) fluctuated between 20-28 per cent, and, the coefficient of variation (around the unweighted average of wage rates in 26 industries) ranged between 14-16 per cent. A linear trend regression on the coefficient of variation in wage rates during 1952-1970 indicated that the relative dispersion was stable around 15.1 per cent.[6] There was no significant time trend in the year-to-year fluctuations in the coefficient of variation.

Although the overall inter-industry wage differentials were almost unchanged during 1952-1970, the percentage spread in mean wage rates of industries which were on the extremes of the wage structure in 1952 narrowed considerably. The last column of Table 4 shows that in 1952 the average wage rates in the 8 highest paying industries were 43 per cent higher than the wage rates in industries on the bottom of the wage hierarchy. By 1970 some of these industries had regressed towards the

---

5 See Reder, "Wage Differentials," p. 283.

6 The estimated equation for the trend line was as follows:

$$Y_t = 15.16 - \underset{(-0.302)}{0.009X}$$

where Y_t represents the coefficient of variation in wage rates during 1952-1970; X measures the time. Figure in brackets shows the t-value of the trend coefficient. The equation shows that the time trend in relative wage differentials was small and statistically insignificant.

centre of the wage distribution. As a consequence, the percentage wage spread in these two groups of industries was reduced to 25 per cent.

The divergence in the behaviour of overall wage dispersion and the dispersion of wage rates in the 8 highest and 8 lowest paying industries of 1952 indicates that although there was a significant improvement in the relative wage attractiveness of some low wage industries (like bakeries and furniture), the change was too slow and too isolated to have any noticeable impact on the overall inter-industry wage structure.

Inter-Industry Differentials in Wage Rates of Unskilled Labour: A Summary The examination of hourly wage rates of unskilled labourers in 26 manufacturing industries reveals that significant differentials in wage rates exist for this occupation and have persisted for nearly two decades since 1952. The conclusion is based on the following findings.

First, the relative wage hierarchy of industries in 1970 is almost similar to 1952. The stability in the inter-industry wage structure is manifested in very high positive, and statistically significant, coefficients of product-moment correlation between wage rates in 1952 and 1970 and in all pairs of years during this period.

Secondly, in those industries where hourly wages are higher, cents-per-hour wage increases are larger and percentage wage increases smaller than other industries. In other words, cents-per-hour wage improvements are flat rate as well as initial wage level related. Because wage increases are higher in industries already paying higher wage rates, there is little change in the relative wage hierarchy of industries.

Thirdly, although the cents-per-hour differentials in wage rates in 1970 are nearly twice that of 1952, the relative wage differentials are almost unchanged. The coefficient of wage variation, a measure of relative wage differentials, is 15 per cent and has remained nearly constant since 1952; year-to-year fluctuations in the coefficient are small and do not show any secular trend.

Although the overall inter-industry wage differentials have been persistent, the percentage differentials in mean wage rates between industries on the upper and lower extremes of the wage structure have narrowed. The divergent behaviour of overall inter-industry wage dispersion and percentage wage differentials between industries on the top and bottom of the wage hierarchy indicates that the changes in relative wage position of industries are too weak and slow to have any noticeable impact on the inter-industry wage structure.

Inter-Industry Differentials in Wage Rates of Skilled Mechanics and in Average Hourly Earnings[7]

Significant inter-industry differentials also exist for skilled workers. Table 5 shows the wage rates of maintenance mechanics, a skilled occupation, in our sample of 26 industries for 1961 and 1970, the period for which data are available. It reveals that over the 10 year period, 1961-1970, there was very little change in the relative wage position on industries for maintenance mechanics. The stability in the inter-industry wage structure for skilled mechanics is further confirmed by the product-moment coefficients of correlation in their wage rates between 1961-1970 (the coefficients are shown in the upper half of Table 6). The indexes of absolute and relative differentials in wage rates of maintenance mechanics in Table 6 indicate that while absolute cents-per-hour differentials in their wage rates nearly doubled during 1961-1970, the relative wage differentials remained almost the same, in the range of 12-13 per cent (except for 1970 when they jumped to 15.9 per cent). Thus, the analysis of wage rates of skilled mechanics shows that significant wage differentials also exist for skilled mechanics and have been persistent for the past 10 years at least.

Table 5, which shows the wage rates of maintenance mechanics, also gives the average hourly earnings of all production workers in our sample of 26 manufacturing industries. It discloses that the relative average hourly earnings of all production workers are high in those industries where relative wage rates of maintenance mechanics are high (a comparison of Table 5 with Table 1 suggests that the same industries also pay high relative wages to unskilled workers). Furthermore, Table 6 shows that like the relative wage position of unskilled labourers and maintenance mechanics, the relative position of all production workers (including unskilled and skilled workers) in average hourly earnings was also almost unchanged during 1961-1970. Similarly the coefficient of variation in average hourly earnings during this period also did not show any significant change (see lower right hand column of Table 6).

---

7 Maintenance mechanics' wages are straight time wage rates, similar to unskilled labour wage rates, taken from *Wage Rates, Salaries and Hours of Labour* (Ottawa: Information Canada, Annual). The average hourly earnings are gross payments to all workers in an industry before deductions are made for taxes, unemployment insurance etc. They include straight time wages, overtime wages, cost of living allowances, holiday, sickness and vacation pay as well as regularly paid bonuses. Average hourly earnings are calculated by dividing the total wage bill by the total manhours. The data were obtained from the Statistics Canada publication, *Manufacturing Industries of Canada*, Cat. No. 31-203 (Ottawa: Information Canada, Annual).

Table 5

Inter-Industry Structure of Wage Rates for Maintenance Mechanics and of Average Hourly Earnings of all Production Workers

Industry	Wage rates of maintenance mechanics				Average hourly earnings			
	Hourly rate ($)		Relative wage*		In $		Relative rate*	
	1961	1970	1961	1970	1961	1970	1961	1970
Furniture	1.66	2.81	75	76	1.46	2.40	74	73
Bakeries	1.92	3.54	87	96	1.50	2.56	76	78
Biscuits	2.11	3.62	96	98	1.37	2.47	69	76
Paper boxes & bags	2.03	3.33	92	90	1.68	2.89	85	88
Dairy factories	1.88	3.14	85	85	1.50	2.84	76	87
Leather tanneries	1.82	2.85	83	77	1.84	2.69	93	82
Pharmaceuticals	2.07	3.28	94	89	1.56	2.48	79	76
Rubber products	2.11	3.51	96	95	1.88	3.13	95	96
Office & store machinery	2.29	3.18	104	86	2.19	3.59	111	110
Machine shops	2.04	3.34	93	90	1.68	3.07	85	94
Aircraft & parts	2.02	4.06	92	110	2.11	3.50	107	107
Veneer mills	1.84	3.40	84	92	1.67	3.03	84	93
Agricultural implements	2.32	3.91	105	106	2.20	3.47	111	106
Metal stamping, etc.	2.08	3.72	95	100	2.02	3.15	102	96
Small electric appliances	2.16	3.17	98	86	1.77	2.56	89	78
Industrial electric equipment	2.35	3.48	107	94	2.10	3.12	106	96
Breweries	2.61	4.55	119	123	2.34	3.88	118	119
Tobacco products	2.42	4.47	110	121	1.92	3.64	97	112
Iron foundries	2.25	3.38	102	92	1.94	3.32	98	102
Pulp & paper	2.50	4.02	114	109	2.35	3.77	119	116
Meat packing	2.19	3.61	100	98	2.00	3.24	101	99
Industrial chemicals	2.41	3.97	109	107	2.35	3.80	119	116
Petroleum refineries	2.61	4.41	119	119	2.60	4.25	131	130
Motor vehicle parts	2.34	4.41	106	119	2.21	3.52	112	108
Iron & steel mills	2.68	4.04	122	109	2.55	3.86	129	118
Motor vehicle assembly	2.58	4.89	117	132	2.36	4.06	119	124
Unweighted average	2.20	3.70	100	100	1.97	3.25	100	100

* Relative rates are the ratio of each industry's wage rate or hourly earnings and the unweighted average of all industries multiplied by 100.

Table 6

Inter-Temporal Correlation and Dispersion in Wage Rates of Unskilled Labour, Maintenance Mechanics and in Average Hourly Earnings of Production Workers

Years correlated	Coefficient of correlation: Wages of unskilled labour	Wages of maintenance mechanics	Average hourly earnings
1961:1962	0.98*	0.94*	0.99*
1961:1965	0.93*	0.90*	0.98*
1961:1968	0.86*	0.82*	0.95*
1961:1970	0.90*	0.80*	0.92*
1965:1968	0.94*	0.90*	0.99*
1965:1970	0.93*	0.88*	0.96*
1968:1970	0.91*	0.88*	0.97*

Absolute and relative dispersion

	Standard deviation (in cents per hour)			Coefficient of variation (per cent)		
Years	Unskilled labour wages	Wages of mainte-nance mechanics	Average hourly earnings	Wages of unskilled labour	Wages of mainte-nance mechanics	Average hourly earnings
1961	27	27	35	16.2	12.3	17.8
1962	27	28	36	15.7	12.0	17.7
1963	28	30	37	15.6	12.6	17.7
1964	29	29	37	15.7	12.0	17.1
1965	30	32	38	15.8	12.4	16.7
1966	32	35	41	15.8	13.0	17.0
1967	33	37	42	15.3	12.8	16.5
1968	34	41	45	14.5	13.0	16.2
1969	36	45	47	14.2	13.0	15.6
1970	39	59	52	14.1	15.9	16.0

* Statistically significant at the .01 probalility level.

The similarity in relative wage position of unskilled workers and maintenance mechanics and in average hourly earnings of all production workers in 26 Canadian manufacturing industries suggests that some industries in Canada pay more than the others to all their workers, irrespective of their skill level. This similarity is further demonstrated by the statistically significant association between wage rates of unskilled workers, wage rates of skilled maintenance mechanics and average hourly earnings of all production workers. Table 7 gives the coefficients of correlation in wage rates for workers in the two occupational categories and average hourly earnings. The high positive correlation in wage rates of unskilled labourers and maintenance mechanics indicates that in those industries where wage rates of skilled workers are higher than other industries, unskilled workers also receive a high relative wage. The high correlation in wage rates of unskilled workers, wage rates of maintenance mechanics and average hourly earnings shows that some industries in general pay better than others.

Table 7

The Relationship Between Wage Rates of Unskilled Labour, Skilled Mechanics and Average Hourly Earnings

	Coefficients of correlation in wage rates of		
Year	Unskilled labour and skilled mechanics	Unskilled labour and average hourly earnings	Skilled mechanics and average hourly earnings
1961	0.92*	0.84*	0.85*
1962	0.91*	0.85*	0.81*
1963	0.86*	0.82*	0.75*
1964	0.86*	0.83*	0.79*
1965	0.90*	0.82*	0.81*
1966	0.70*	0.77*	0.75*
1967	0.73*	0.74*	0.77*
1968	0.77*	0.82*	0.77*
1969	0.87*	0.76*	0.79*
1970	0.86*	0.76*	0.81*

* Statistically significant at the .001 probability level.

Relationship Between Wage Rates and Wage Supplements

Although wage rates do not fully measure total monetary returns to labour for services, they can be approximated to total compensation or total pecuniary rewards. The approximation is based on the assumption that the non-wage benefits, commonly referred to as fringe benefits or employee benefits, are distributed proportionately to wages. The validity of this assumption can be tested by examining the relationship between the monetary value of fringe benefits and straight-time earnings of production workers in two-digit manufacturing industries in Canada, for which estimates are available.[8] The estimated relationship can be generalised for our industry sample[9] and for differences in pecuniary rewards for workers of similar skill in view of our finding that the inter-industry wage structures for unskilled labour and for skilled maintenance mechanics are similar to the inter-industry structure of earnings.

Table 8 shows that the value of wage supplements ranges between 17 cents in knitting to $1.02 in the petroleum industry. The supplements are lower in industries where straight-time earnings are low, and higher in high wage industries. The coefficient of product-moment correlation between wage supplements and straight-time earnings is 0.95, statistically significant at the .01 probability level. An ordinary least squares regression of the value of wage supplements on straight-time earnings revealed that 89 per cent of the total inter-industry variations in the value of wage supplements are due to differentials in straight-time earnings across industries.[10]

---

8 The estimates are derived from the *Survey of Labour Costs in Manufacturing*, Cat. No. 72-510 (Ottawa: Dominion Bureau of Statistics, 1968). Total cost of employee benefits in the survey includes premium pay for overtime, holidays and shift work, vacation and sick pay, miscellaneous direct payments, employer contributions to workmen's compensation, unemployment insurance, public and private pension plans, life insurance and health plans.

9 Our sample of 26 industries forms part of the 20 two-digit manufacturing groups for which data are available. The relationship between wages and fringe benefits in aggregate groups should therefore be applicable to our sample, at least on a cross-section basis.

10 The estimate of the regression is as follows:

$$Y_i = \underset{(-6.45)^*}{-60.29} + \underset{(12.45)^*}{50.15X_i} \qquad \bar{R}^2 = 0.89$$

where Y_i is cents-per-hour value of wage supplements and X_i is the level of straight-time earnings ($i = 1 \ldots 20$). Figures in parenthesis are t-values of the coefficients and * denotes statistical significance at the .01 probability level.

Table 8

Inter-Industry Differences in Earnings and Wage Supplements

Industry groups	Straight time earnings per hour ($)	Value of wage supple-ments ($)	Total labour cost ($)	Supple-ments as a per cent of labour cost
Food & beverages	2.13	0.44	2.57	17.1
Tobacco	2.47	0.71	3.18	22.3
Rubber	2.36	0.75	3.11	24.1
Leather	1.76	0.25	2.01	12.4
Textiles	1.85	0.38	2.23	17.0
Knitting	1.45	0.17	1.62	10.5
Clothing	1.56	0.21	1.77	11.9
Wood	2.12	0.37	2.49	14.8
Furniture	1.82	0.29	2.11	13.7
Paper & allied industries	2.65	0.67	3.32	20.2
Printing	2.69	0.60	3.29	18.2
Primary metal	2.80	0.81	3.61	22.4
Metal fabricating	2.30	0.49	2.79	17.6
Machinery	2.58	0.66	3.44	19.2
Transportation equipment	2.74	0.92	3.66	25.1
Electric products	2.32	0.51	2.83	18.0
Non-metallic mineral products	2.48	0.58	3.06	18.9
Petroleum	3.14	1.02	4.16	24.5
Chemicals	2.50	0.64	3.14	20.4
Miscellaneous	2.02	0.41	2.43	16.8

The table also shows that the inter-industry differentials in wage supplements are larger than the differentials in straight-time earnings (the coefficient of variation in supplements is 42.1 per cent compared with the 19 per cent variation in straight-time earnings). The larger differentials in wage supplements tend to make for a larger variation in total compensation, i.e., 23.0 per cent, than the variation in earnings.

The analysis indicates that the structure of earnings is a good approximation of the inter-industry differentials in pecuniary rewards of labour or the price of labour per unit of time. Given the high correlation between average hourly earnings and wage rates of unskilled and skilled labour, this approximation can also be considered representative of the differentials in the price of labour of similar skill across industries.

Conclusion

In Canada, some industries pay higher wage rates than others to workers of similar skill: significant inter-industry differentials exist for unskilled labour as well as for skilled workers. In the industries where wage rates for skilled labour are higher, unskilled workers also receive higher wage rates, and the average hourly earnings of all production workers are more than the industry average.

In the case of unskilled labour the inter-industry differentials have been persistent for nearly two decades since 1952. There has been little change in the relative position of industries in the inter-industry wage hierarchy.

The wage supplements in industries depend upon the level of earnings: the wage supplements (in cents-per-hour) are larger in industries where hourly earnings are higher. The finding suggests that inter-industry wage differentials can be considered approximately representative of the differentials in total pecuniary rewards or to differences in monetary returns to labour of similar skill.

The evidence of persistent wage differentials for workers of similar skill has important implications for the competitive wage theory, which, abstracting from the compensating differentials in non-pecuniary attributes of employment, predicts equalization in the price of labour of the same skill level. In the background of these findings the validity of the competitive theory hinges on the compensating differentials in non-pecuniary aspects of employment between industries.

3
Determinants of Inter-Industry Wage Differentials

The examination of wage rates of unskilled labourers and of maintenance mechanics, in the preceding chapter, demonstrated that some industries in Canada persistently pay higher wages than others to workers of equal skill. In this chapter we attempt to explain why wage rates for apparently similar jobs differ between industries. Using an integrated relative wage determination model we study whether, and to what extent, differentials in wage rates compensate for the differences in non-pecuniary attributes of employment, whether relative wages are higher in unionized industries than in non-unionized industries, whether large firms in an industry pay a wage premium to all workers or only to skilled workers, and what is the impact of unions on wage rates in industries where a few big firms account for a significant proportion of total employment and output.

The first section presents a brief outline of the long run competitive theory of wage differentials and the institutional wage model, and provides a rationale for an integrated approach to relative wage determination. We analyze the relevant non-pecuniary factors cited by Adam Smith in defence of wage differentials, investigate the mechanism of union influence on relative wage rates and inquire into the relationship among market factors, degree of unionization and the concentration of large firms in the product market.

The second section develops a conceptual framework for inter-industry wage determination, in which wage rates for workers of similar skill are dependent upon the non-pecuniary aspects of employment, the extent of unionization and the degree of large firm concentration in the product market. The third section specifies the variables of the model outlined in the second section. The fourth section contains the empirical results of our model for both unskilled labour and skilled mechanics. A summary of the results and their implications is provided in the last section.

Factors in Wage Differentials

The Long Run Competitive Wage Model

According to the competitive theory an industry under competitive conditions will pay the same price for a homogeneous grade of labour as any other industry hiring in the same location, abstracting from difference in non-pecuniary aspects of employment. The theory predicts equalization of net advantages to similar grades of labour across industries, where net advantages include both pecuniary (meaning monetary returns) and non-pecuniary rewards. Assuming an infinitely elastic supply of labour to each industry[1] in the long run, inter-industry differences in wage rates[2] for a similar grade of labour reflect the compensating differences in non-pecuniary aspects of employment between industries.

An important implication of the competitive model is that, because of the infinitely elastic supply of labour to each industry in the long run, differentials in wage rates for a homogeneous grade of labour between industries are determined purely by supply conditions (or by differences in non-pecuniary aspects of industries), and are not affected by shifts in demand for labour. Figure A illustrates the situation.

The figure shows the supply and demand curves for a homogeneous grade of labour in industries i and j. Whereas the supply curves S_i and S_j determine wage rates W_i and W_j, demand curves D_i and D_j determine employment N_i and N_j in the ith and j^{th} industries. The difference in wage rates (W_i-W_j) between two industries relates to differences in the height of the two supply curves. Since the differences in supply curves reflect compensating differentials in non-pecuniary attributes of industries, industry i pays a higher wage rate because it is less attractive in non-pecuniary aspects of employment compared to industry j. In the framework of competitive theory although the two industries pay differ-

1 The assumption of an infinitely elastic supply curve of labour implies that all workers have similar assessment of the non-pecuniary attributes of different industries. For evidence that long run labour supply elasticities are in fact very large see T. W. McGuire and L. A. Rapping, "The Role of Market Variables and Key Bargains in the Manufacturing Wage Determination Process," *Journal of Political Economy* 76 (September-October, 1968): 1015-1036 and H. G. Lewis, *Unionism and Relative Wages*, p. 23.

2 Wage rates are treated analogously to total pecuniary rewards or price of labour. By definition the price of labour includes wage rates and pecuniary employee benefits. It was pointed out in the previous chapter that employee benefits are wage related, i.e., the higher the wage the higher the cost of employee benefits. The relationship suggested that wage rates could be treated as a proxy to price of labour or to total pecuniary rewards for an hour of labour services, at least in a cross-section analysis.

ent wage rates, the "net advantage" to workers (of similar skills) is equal because of the compensating differentials in non-pecuniary aspects of employment.

Figure A

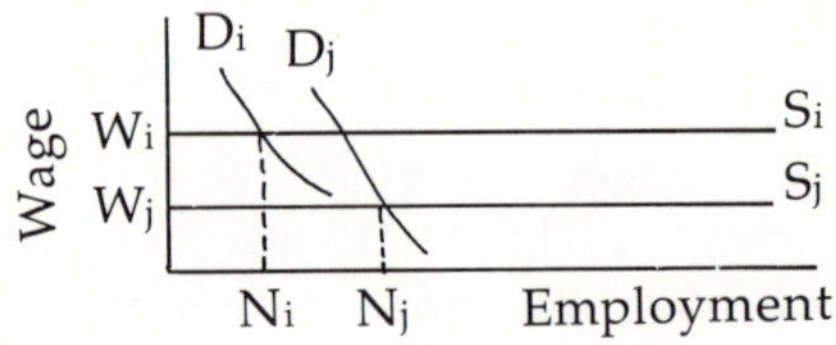

Important Non-Pecuniary Aspects of Employment According to Adam Smith,[3] in whose writings the basic ideas of the competitive theory of wage differentials originated, five non-pecuniary aspects of employment mainly compensate for differences in pecuniary rewards: agreeableness of employment (ease, cleanliness, honourableness of employment); cost of learning; constancy of employment; degree of trust (responsibility required in handling equipment and material); probability of success.

Although Adam Smith outlined these five factors to explain "inequities" in earnings between occupations, they "can be used to explain differences in wages within an occupation between employers, between industries and between locations."[4] For the explanation of inter-industry differentials in wage rates for workers of similar skill only two, agreeableness of employment and the constancy of employment, of the five factors mentioned by Smith are relevant; the other three factors — cost of learning, degree of responsibility required in handling equipment and material, and the probability of success or the degree of financial risk in training for a profession — are important factors in skill differentials but not in wage differentials for workers of similar skill. The cost of learning refers to the cost and time involved in education and training. Differences in these costs give rise to earning differentials

3 Adam Smith, *Wealth of Nations*, Vol. I, Chapter X, pp. 111-119.

4 Rees, *Compensating Wage Differentials*, p. 2. According to Rees, "of the many ideas of Adam Smith that have stood the test of time, few have weathered better or are still more relevant than the idea of compensating wage differentials." The best defence of Adam Smith's ideas is found in Alfred Marshall, *Principles of Economics*, 8th edition (London: Macmillan, 1962), pp. 454-464.

between occupational groups.[5] However, the cost of training for an occupation is presumed to be the same. Similarly, workers of similar skill have generally the same level of responsibility in every industry, even though the type of equipment and materials may differ between industries in weight, danger, risk and value. The probability of success factor applies to professions like acting and singing where there are considerable financial uncertainties related to the career. These professions have a remote possibility of big financial rewards and high risks of failures.

The two non-pecuniary factors applicable to the explanation of inter-industry wage differentials for similar work, agreeableness of employment and constancy of employment, primarily relate to the nature and conditions of work, and to the location of industries. The agreeableness of employment refers to the arduousness and hazards of work. This is evident from the example Smith gave to illustrate the nature of agreeableness of an employment:

> . . . a journeyman blacksmith, although an artificer, seldom earns so much in twelve hours as a collier, who is only a labourer, does in eight because his work is not quite so dirty, is less dangerous and is carried out in day-light, and above ground.[6]

The implication of the argument is that a worker will accept a lower wage of one industry than the other if work in the low wage industry is less physically strenuous, less hazardous and performed in pleasant surroundings.

The constancy or inconstancy of employment, as a non-pecuniary factor cited by Smith, relates to workers' preference for a secure job in an industry where there is little or no risk of seasonal unemployment and frequent layoffs. He gave the following example:

> In the greater part of manufactures, a journeyman may be pretty sure of employment almost every day in the year that he is able to work. A mason or bricklayer, on the contrary, can work neither in hard frost nor in foul weather, and his employment at all other times depends upon the occasional calls of his customers. He is liable in consequence to be frequently without any. What he earns, therefore, while he is employed, must not only maintain him while he is idle, but make him some compensation for those anxious and

5 For a modern treatment of the subject see Gary S. Becker, *Human Capital* (New York: National Bureau of Economic Research, 1966), pp. 7-36.

6 Smith, *Wealth of Nations*, p. 112.

desponding moments which the thought of so precarious a situation must sometimes occasion.[7]

The example suggests that wage rates would be higher in the construction industry than in manufacturing, or more generally in an industry where employment is more seasonal and cyclically instable.

A third non-pecuniary factor, not specifically cited by Smith but most relevant to the explanation of wage differentials for similar work, relates to strong preferences of workers towards particular regions and geographical areas. These preferences may stem from social reasons or from pure economic reasons. For example, if wage rates are historically higher in one region than the other, workers may demand higher wage rates in the high wage region.

Briefly then, we can interpret the competitive theory as saying that wage differentials for a similar grade of labour may persist in the long run if there are compensating non-pecuniary differentials related to onerousness of work, work hazard, location, and the seasonal and cyclical stability of employment.

The Institutional Hypothesis

The institutional wage model emphasizes the significant role of trade unions and large oligopolistic firms in relative wage determination. It maintains that wage rates for a worker of equal skill are higher in unionized and oligopolistic industries than in non-unionized competitive industries.

Economic theory concedes a possible union influence on wage structure in the short run, due to factors such as the inelasticity of demand for union labour and because of union imposed work rules and regulations which may restrict the supply of labour and impede factor substitution.[8]

---

7 *Ibid.*, p. 115-116.

8 Alfred Marshall, *Principles Of Economics*, pp. 318-20; Milton Friedman, *Price Theory: A Provisional Text*, pp. 155-159; and Lloyd Ulman, "Marshall and Friedman on Union Strength," *Review of Economics and Statistics* 37 (November, 1955): 384-401. Marshall listed four conditions that shape the demand for union labour: elasticity of demand for the product, proportion of union labour in labour force, cost of union labour in total cost of production, and the elasticity of factors of production other than labour. These conditions reflect upon the possibilities of factor substitution and the consumer substitution of final product produced by union labour, and the degree of product price increase due to increase in the price of labour. While these conditions apply to craft unions they can be extended to the influence of industrial unions if industrial unions cover a significant portion of thé industry labour force.

In the long run, however, union relative wage effects for workers of similar skill should be insignificant because of the factor substitution and changes in the techniques of production.[9]

Though inconsistent with the predictions of economic theory there is considerable empirical evidence supporting a permanent union impact on relative wage rates for workers of similar skill.[10] The empirical union-nonunion wage differential is generally rationalized on three grounds.[11] First, the wage differential continues because labour markets never fully adjust. The union influence on relative wage rates, in this sense, can be considered as a disequilibrium phenomenon. Secondly, unions are able to secure permanent wage gains by erecting mobility barriers. The union negotiated seniority rules, pension rights, supplementary unemployment benefits and contract provisions relating to loss of jobs on account of technical change are often quoted as barriers to mobility. Thirdly, the presence of large firms controlling the industry product market provide a permissive environment for a steady union influence on relative wage rates.

The notion that large firms pay higher wage rates than small firms, and that unions are more effective in industries dominated by large firms than in competitive industries, is not obvious in economic theory based on the assumption of profit maximization. If anything, the theory might suggest a low wage, below the competitive level, in monopolistic and oligopolistic industries where a few large firms account for a major proportion of the total industry employment and output.[12]

Profit maximization, however, may not be an ideal assumption in analyzing the behaviour of large firms. It is sometimes argued that oligopolistic companies, because of their high profitability are very conscious of their public image. They might pay higher wage rates to win public approval. It has also been suggested that large firms may conspire with unions in using wage rates as a barrier to entry by imposing high

---

9 Rees, *Economics of Trade Unions*, pp. 69-99.

10 See Lewis, *Unionism and Relative Wages*; Weiss, "Concentration"; Cohen, *Determinants of Supply and Demand;* Reber, *Effects of Unionism*; and Rosen, "Occupational Wage Structure".

11 The three arguments are discussed in Rees, *Economics of Trade Unions*; Holt, "Job Search"; Levinson, "Unionism, Concentration and Wage Changes"; and M. Segal, "Union Wage Impact and Market Wage Structure," *Quarterly Journal of Economics* 78 (February, 1964): 96-114.

12 See Rees, *Economics of Trade Unions*, pp. 82-87, and "Union Gains and Enterprise Monopoly," in *Essays on Industrial Relations Research* (Ann Arbor: Institute of Labor and Industrial Relations, the University of Michigan-Wayne State University, 1961).

wages on other firms in an industry. A prominent economist, for example, remarks that

> . . . it may be profitable for existing firms to tolerate high wages as long as these are enforced by a union strong enough to impose the same wage scale on new entrants.[13]

A necessary condition for wage rates to act as a barrier to entry of new firms in an industry is that an increase in wage rates should produce a differential shift in the level of average costs to the relative disadvantage of small firms. This is possible when there are systematic differences in technology, particularly in the capital-labour ratio, between successive scales of operation.[14]

Recent research has indicated that large firms may pay higher wages to skilled workers than small firms for greater selectivity in recruiting and for stable attachment — the main reason being the higher cost of search, hiring and training of skilled labour than of the unskilled labour for whom these costs are considered negligible.[15] The cost of successful skill search is said to be substantially higher for large firms than for small companies who may directly observe the quality of new workers and, therefore, need not resort to expensive and sometimes uncertain practices of estimating workers' performance. Employers in large firms may pay higher relative wages to reduce these costs: not only is the quit rate of existing skilled workers reduced by high wage rates, but on average, the employer has less difficulty in attracting qualified workers from other firms.[16]

Unions may be more effective in large firms because of their ability to erect mobility barriers and to reduce quit rates.[17] They may thus help employers seeking a lower quit rate of skilled workers, and potential restrictions on entry of new firms. Large firms, generally characterized by plants employing a large number of workers, may indirectly provide

---

13 Franco Modigliani, "New Developments on the Oligopoly Front," *Journal of Political Economy* 56 (June, 1958): 288, n. 21.

14 For a theoretical model of wage rates as a barrier to entry see Oliver E. Williamson, "Wage Rates as a Barrier to Entry: The Pennington Case in Perspective," *Quarterly Journal Of Economics* 83 (February, 1968): 85-116.

15 See Oi, "Labor as a Quasi-fixed Factor"; Weiss, "Concentration".

16 See Stigler, "Labour Market", pp. 101-103.

17 Average mobility rates have been found to be less in unionized industries than in non-unionized industries. For Canadian evidence, see Vanderkamp, *Mobility Behaviour*, pp. 57-80. Vanderkamp found that average mobility rates varied inversely with the percentage of workers covered by collective agreements.

conditions necessary for the effective functioning of unions. The servicing of union workers is presumed to be less expensive in large plants than in small plants. The organization of large firms in an industry by a union also provides a benefit to unskilled workers, especially if they are organized on industry lines rather than on craft lines, in that industrial unions are known to pursue a policy of equitable internal wage differentials marked by equitable wage increases for all workers — skilled or unskilled. Thus, unions may push up wage rates of unskilled and semi-skilled workers in industries where wage rates of skilled labour are relatively high for one reason or another. Raimon, for example, has argued that:

> The trade unions have sought to force the money wage level of the firm to the height necessary to recruit or to retain workers in the occupational categories in shortest supply through insistence on the maintenance of intraplant 'equities' in occupational wage relationships. This is perhaps the most significant achievement of American unionism in the wage field.[18]

He suggests that:

> . . . industries with a relatively high proportion of occupationally hired skilled labour are more vulnerable to the 'inequity' stratagem and thus may be forced to pay higher rates than other industries for their semi-skilled and unskilled labour.[19]

The "equity" policy is manifested in a high positive relationship between the degree of unionization and the percentage differential between skilled and unskilled labour wage rates. In short, in non-unionized large firms only skilled labour wages would be higher, but with unionization, wages for all workers may be higher in large firms than in small firms.

The high relative wage rates resulting from the unionization of large firms imply an industrial segmentation of the labour market; according to Hildebrand and Delhanty, wage rates in the top segment of industries move mainly with the union settlements that tie the unskilled labour wage to skilled labour wage despite any relative competitive advantage and overall conditions of labour supply in the ranks of unskilled labour.

---

18 Raimon, "Indeterminateness of Wages," pp. 182-183.

19 *Ibid.*, p. 183, n. 15.

The workers in the bottom segment of industries receive a competitive wage and are influenced by changes in the labour market.[20] This industrial segmentation is reflected in the stability of quit rates among industries and the negative association between quit rates and wage rates, degree of unionization and the degree of concentration in the product market.[21]

Integrated Competitive-Institutional Wage Model

Although the competitive market model and the institutional approach to wage differentials are commonly treated as alternative models of wage determination, they may be integrated into one model, at least for explaining the inter-industry differentials in wage rates for workers of equal skill.[22] There are many reasons why this integration is desirable.

Since collective bargaining for wages and working conditions is a marked feature of the labour market in manufacturing industries, it may not be reasonable to contend that unions do not exert any influence on relative wage rates for workers of similar skill even though competitive forces may be powerful. The stability in industry quit rates over time and the inverse association between the degree of unionization and quit rates appear to indicate that union-imposed barriers to mobility may be strong and effective.

The product market may be partially, but not fully, competitive on account of large firms employing a significant fraction of the total workforce and accounting for a large proportion of total output. Large firms may pay higher wage rates for greater selectivity in recruiting and to create barriers to entry of new firms in an industry.

The institutional influence of unions and large firms may not be

---

20 See G. H. Hildebrand and G. E. Delhanty, "Wage Levels and Differentials," in *Prosperity and Unemployment*, eds. R. Gordon and M. Gordon (New York: John Wiley, 1966), pp. 265-301. Hildebrand and Delhanty maintain that the unskilled workers have a competitive disadvantage to skilled workers, because while a skilled worker can replace an unskilled worker, the unskilled worker can not be substituted for skilled workers. They also argue that unskilled labour has been in relative excess supply since the beginning of the 1960's.

21 See John Pencavel, *An Analysis of the Quit Rate in American Manufacruting Industries* (Princeton: Industrial Relations Section, Princeton University, 1970); and Robert V. Eagly, "Market Power as an Intervening Mechanism in Phillips Curve Analysis," *Economica* 32 (February, 1965): 48-64.

22 According to Rees "a full understanding of wage structure involves both market and non-market institutions, and to ignore either one will result in incomplete explanations." See Rees, *Compensating Wage Differentials.*

independent of market forces. In the absence of unions, the competitive wage differentials are explained by reference to labour supply conditions or the non-pecuniary attributes of employment. If conditions of work in an industry are unattractive, premium wage rates must be paid to attract an adequate labour supply. Unions, by influencing both wage rates and working conditions, may reduce the need for such premiums.[23] In North America, unions are generally credited for better safety rules, job security, protection from technological displacement, rationing lay-offs, improved grievance procedures, shorter hours of work, reduced absenteeism etc. This may be the reason why voluntary labour mobility is less in unionized industries than in non-unionized industries.

An integrated model of relative wage determination would take account of both the market factors and the non-market institutional factors.

Analytical Framework

Relative Wages and Non-Pecuniary Aspects

Under competitive conditions, where the long run supply curve of labour to each industry is considered to be infinitely elastic, inter-industry differentials in wage rates for a homogeneous grade of labour should reflect compensating differentials in non-pecuniary attributes of industry employment. Let P_i be an index of the degree of unpleasantness of non-pecuniary aspects of employment in the ith industry paying a wage rate W_{ci}. (P_i will be negative for a pleasant non-pecuniary characteristic, and positive for unpleasantness.) The competitive wage theory predicts that $W_{ci}/(1+P_i)$ will be the same in all industries. Define the long run competitive equilibrium wage rate as W_c. Then,

(1) $W_c = W_{ci}/(1+P_i)$ or

(1a) $W_{ci} = W_c(1+P_i)$

According to equation (1a) the competitive wage rate, W_{ci}, is equal to the equilibrium wage rate W_c grossed up to compensate for the unpleasantness of the non-pecuniary attributes of the ith industry.

23 James R. Schlesinger, "Market Structure, Union Power and Inflation," in *Labor and Trade Unionism*, eds. Walter Galenson and Seymore Martin Lipset (New York: John Wiley, 1960), pp. 155-169; and Albert Rees, "Some Non-Wage Aspects of Collective Bargaining", in *The Public Stake in Union Power*, ed. Philip Bradley (Charlottesville: University of Virginia Press, 1969), pp. 124-142.

Relative Wage Rates and Unionization

Representing W_i^u and W_i^n as the union and non-union wage rates respectively in the ith industry, the relative wage advantage of a union over a non-union worker (assumed constant) can be defined as

$$k = (W_i^u - W_i^n)/W_i^n \equiv (W_i^u/W_i^n) - 1$$

The union wage rate in the ith industry will be as follows:

$$(2) \quad W_i^u = (1+k)\, W_i^n$$

The observed wage rate for a homogeneous grade of labour, W_i^*, can be taken as a weighted mean of the union and non-union wage rates:

$$(3) \quad W_i^* = U_i . W_i^u + (1 - U_i)\, W_i^n$$

where U_i is the proportion of union workers in the ith industry.

It is further assumed that the non-union wage rate could differ from the competitive wage rate, but this difference, if present, is assumed to be the same in every industry,[24] i.e.,

$$d = (W_i^n - W_{ci}) / W_{ci} \equiv (W_i^n/W_{ci}) - 1$$

The relationship between W_{ci} and W_i^n can be expressed as,

$$(4) \quad W_i^n = (1+d)\, W_{ci}$$

The relationship between the observed wage rate in i^{th} industry, W_i^*, a weighted average of the union and non-union wage rates, and the competitive wage rate, W_{ci}, can be derived by first inserting (2) into (3) and then substituting (4) into (3). Inserting (2) into (3) gives:

$$(5) \quad W_i^* = U_i\, (1+k)\, W_i^n + (1 - U_i)\, W_i^n \text{ or}$$

---

24 The non-union wage rate W_i^n may differ from the competitive wage rate W_{ci} for two reasons. First, the higher union wage rate in one part of the industry may bring about contraction of employment. The wages in the non-union sector of the industry may thus be bid below the competitive wage rate. Secondly, the threat of unionization may force employers to raise wages above the competitive wage rate. See Lewis, "Unionism and Relative Wages", pp.18-27.

(6) $W_i = W_i^n[U_i(1+k) + (1-U_i)]$ or

(7) $W_i^* = W_i^n(1+kU_i)$

Now substituting (4) for W_i^n,

(8) $W_i^* = W_{ci}(1+d)(1+kU_i)$

Relative Wage Rates and the Structure of the Product Market

The independent effect of large firms, accounting for a significant portion of an industry's labour force and output, on relative wage rates can be estimated in a manner similar to that used for estimating the union wage premium. Let W_i^m be the wage rate paid by large firms compared to the wage rate W_i^* in small firms, the oligopolistic wage premium (assumed constant) can be defined as $s = (W_i^m - W_i^*)/W_i^*$ or $(W_i^m/W_i^*) - 1$. The relationship between the wage rate in small firms and the wage rate in large firms in industry i can be expressed as follows:

(9) $W_i^m = (1+s) W_i^*$

If industry i contains both the large firms, paying W_i^m, and small firms paying W_i^*, the average industry wage (call it W_i) will be a weighted mean of the two wage rates (weight being the proportion of total labour force in industry i employed by large firms):

(10) $W_i = C_i \cdot W_i^m + (1-C_i) W_i^*$

where C_i is the proportion of workers in i^{th} industry engaged in large firms.

Substituting (9) into (10) gives:

(11) $W_i = C_i(1+s) W_i^* + (1-C_i) W_i^*$ or

(12) $W_i = W_i^*[C_i(1+s) + (1-C_i)]$ or

(13) $W_i = W_i^*(1+sC_i)$

Integrated Model of Relative Wage Determination

Assuming that d, s and k are constants and independent of each other, the competitive theory and the institutional hypotheses can now be integrated into a single model of wage determination. Combining (8) and (13) gives:

$$(14) \quad W_i = W_{ci} [(1+d)(1+kU_i)(1+sC_i)]$$

The equation (14) postulates that the observed wage rate in industry i is equal to the competitive wage rate plus a union wage premium and a large firm wage premium.

The institutional model in (14) can now be integrated with the competitive wage model in (1a). Substituting (1a) into (14) gives:

$$(15) \quad W_i = W_c (1+P_i)(1+d)(1+kU_i)(1+sC_i)$$

The log-linear stochastic form of (15) can be written as follows:

$$(16) \quad \ln W_i = \ln [(1+d)W_c] + \ln (1+P_i) + \ln (1+kU_i) + \ln (1+sC_i) + \ln (1+\varepsilon_i)$$

where ε_i is a random error term.

The equation (16) might reasonably be approximated by the following equation:

$$(17) \quad \ln W_i = \alpha + \beta A_i + kU_i + sC_i + u_i$$

where $\alpha = \ln [(1+d) W_c]$. A_i is a *vector* of measures of non- pecuniary attributes of employment and β a *vector* of coefficients. βA_i is intended to approximate $\ln (1+P_i)$; the terms kU_i and sC_i appear because $kU_i = \ln (1+kU_i)$ and $sC_i = \ln (1+sC_i)$ if both sC_i and kU_i are small. Past evidence[25] for the United States indicates that s and k are less than one, and both U_i and C_i are less than unity by definition, so that the products kU_i and sC_i will almost certainly be small enough for the approximation to be quite adequate. Finally the error term $u_i = \ln (1+ \varepsilon_i)$.

The estimating equation (17) postulates that wage rates for a homogeneous grade of labour in industry i are a function of non-pecuniary attributes of employment, degree of unionization and the degree of large firms' concentration. The expected sign of coefficients of non-pecuniary variables will depend on their specification, as spelled

25 See H. G. Lewis, "The Effects of Unions on Industrial Wage Differentials," in *Aspects of Labor Economics* (New York: N.B.E.R., 1962), pp. 319-344; Weiss, "Concentration," pp. 96-117; and Rosen, "Occupational Wage Structure".

out in the third section, Specification of Variables, below. Our expectations regarding k and s, on the basis of the institutional theory, are not so obvious. As pointed out in the discussion of the institutional theory above, the relative wage effects of unions and large firms may be interrelated and asymmetric for unskilled and skilled labour. We therefore consider the *a priori* expectations on k and s separately for the two occupational categories.

Model of Unskilled Labour Relative Wage Determination

Equation (17) assumed that k and s are constants, independent of each other and of the values of the variables in the equation. However, the union policy of equitable internal wage differentials, discussed above, implies that the union-nonunion differentials for unskilled labour are dependent upon the wage premium paid to skilled labour in large firms. Thus, in the case of unskilled labour the value of k may be sensitive to the degree of large firm concentration in the product market, C_i. A linear dependency would give the following:

$$(18) \quad k = a + bC_i$$

Substituting (18) for k in equation (17) gives,

$$(19) \quad \ln W_{ui} = \alpha + \beta A_i + aU_i + bU_iC_i + sC_i + u_i$$

where W_{ui} is the wage rate of unskilled workers in industry i. If the equitable internal wage differential mechanism is the *only* way that unions can obtain a higher wage rate for unskilled labour in some industries than others, and if this is the reason why wage rates for unskilled workers are high in industries dominated by large firms — the institutional theory suggests that this is the case — we would expect a = o and s = o. Equation (19) will be reduced to the following:

$$(20) \quad \ln W_{ui} = \alpha + \beta A_i + bU_iC_i + u_i$$

Equation (20) appears to be the only theoretically defensible explanation for inter-industry differentials in wage rates for unskilled labour. It should fit as well as formulations outlined in equation (17) or (19).

Model of Skilled Labour Relative Wage Determination

It was argued above that because of the higher cost of search, hiring and training of skilled workers than of unskilled workers, large firms may pay a higher wage to skilled workers than small firms for greater selectivity and stable attachment. On the basis of this theory we expect that the concentration variable, C_i, will have a significant positive effect on skilled labour wage rates in different industries. The theoretical rationale for union relative wage effects is, however, weak in the case of skilled labour. We do not, therefore, expect unionization to be a significant determinant of wage rates of skilled labour, so that we expect to find that for skilled labour $k = o$. We can rewrite equation (17) for skilled labour as below:

$$(21) \quad \ln W_{si} = \alpha + \beta A_i + sC_i + u$$

where W_{si} refers to the wage rate for skilled labour in industry i. Equation (21) should do as well or better than equation (17), (19) and (20).

Estimation Problems

The received procedure is to estimate equations (17) to (21) by the Ordinary Least Squares Regression (OLS). However, some economists have suggested that the degree of unionization in an industry may not be a purely exogenous variable, but an endogenous variable. It is maintained that the extent of unionism is a positive function of wage rates and non-pecuniary attributes of employment, and inversely related to the cost of union organization which can be approximated by the degree of large firm concentration in the industry product market because of the lower cost of union services in oligopolistic industries characterized by large plants and entry barriers.[26] Thus, in addition to equation (17) we might also have the following unionization equation:

$$(22) \quad U_i = b_o + b_1W_i + b_2A_i + b_3C_i + u_i$$

If we introduce the above equation, however, neither equation (17) nor equation (22) can be identified, and no tests can be undertaken at all. Identification of both equations becomes possible only if we drop W_i from equation (22). In that case no estimation problem arises as a result of simultaneity because equations (17) and (22), without W_i, are recursive and can, therefore, both be best estimated by OLS.

---

26 See Dunlop, *Wage Determination Under Trade Unions*, pp. 28-41; Melvin Reder, "Unions and Wages: The Problems of Measurement," *Journal of Political Economy* 73 (1965): 188-196: and Ashenfelter and Johnson, "Unionism, Relative Wages and Labor Quality".

We move next to a discussion of the detailed specification of variables in equations (17), (19), (20) amd (21).

Specification of Variables

Wage Rates Wage rates used in this study, are average straight time wage rates for male unskilled labourers and skilled maintenance mechanics. Wages are averaged over a 10 year period, 1961-1970, to eliminate year to year fluctuations and discontinuities in wage changes in 2 or 3 year collective agreements.

Although the wage rates are averages of rates in 1961-1970, they are representative of the long run equilibrium inter-industry wage structure, at least in the case of unskilled labour (as demonstrated in the previous chapter, wage rates for unskilled labour between 26 industries during 1952-1970 were highly correlated and their relative variance was constant).

Non-Pecuniary Attributes of Industries In the framework of the classical labour market model, outlined in the *Wealth of Nations,* three non-pecuniary aspects are significant in compensating inter-industry wage differentials for workers of equal skill: irregularity of employment, physical hardship, and location mix.

The *irregularity of employment* can be represented by seasonality and cyclical variability in industry employment.

The index of seasonality was calculated for each industry from the monthly employment of wage earners, expressed in index form with average annual employment each year set at 100. From these figures, available for the period 1961-1968, a ratio was calculated, dividing the three months of highest employment by the three months of lowest employment. The seasonality index was computed by substracting one from this ratio and multiplying by 100. The index can be expressed by the following formula:

$$S = \left[\frac{\Sigma N_i}{\Sigma N_j} - 1 \right] 100$$

where ΣN_i stands for the three months of highest employment and ΣN_j for the three months of lowest employment.

The index of cyclical variability was computed from the time series of real domestic product for each industry, available for the period 1957-1970. A least squares time trend was fitted to the annual data. The variance of the regression was used as an index of cyclical variability.

In the absence of any quantitative measure of the intensity of *physical effort* required in similar jobs between industries, the percentage of females in the industry work-force was taken as a proxy for arduousness of work.[27] It was assumed that since women avoid physically hard work, industries employing a high proportion of females are characterized by jobs requiring low physical effort. This could be one reason why men are paid lower wages in industries where the percentage of women is high.

In addition to the above proxy, the physical hardship of employment between industries was also represented by the frequency of industrial accidents. The frequency of accidents is one measure of physical hazards of a job and is considered an important factor in workers' preference for an industry. Since Canadian statistics on industrial accidents are not available, the study uses the American data on the frequency of industrial accidents. It is assumed that the ranking of industries by industrial accident rates in the two countries is similar, even though the absolute level of rates may differ. The industrial accidents data refer to the total number of disabling work injuries for each million manhours worked. The figures for 1961-1969 were averaged to eliminate short run fluctuations.

The frequency of industrial accidents was weighted by the proportion of unskilled labour in each industry because unskilled workers appear to suffer more from accidents than do skilled workers. The uneven incidence of industrial accidents among occupational groups is reflected in the occupational distribution of employment fatality rates. The data suggest that the employment fatality rates for unskilled labour are nearly twice that for the skilled and semi-skilled.[28] The use of average frequency of industrial accidents overstates the role of accidents in compensating wage differentials in those industries where the proportion of unskilled workers is high.[29] The average frequency of accidents was, therefore, divided by the percentage of unskilled workers in each industry to obtain a uniform measure of the physical hazard.

---

27 This proxy is commonly employed by researchers. See Ashenfelter and Johnson, "Unionism, Relative Wages and Labor Quality", p. 497, and Mark Lutz, *The Equilibrium Wage Structure* (Ph.D. Thesis, University of California (Berkeley) 1972).

28 See Table H in *Labour Gazette* (Ottawa: Canada Department of Labour, monthly). The average employment fatality rate per 10,000 workers is 3.5 - 4.00 for unskilled labourers compared to a rate of 1.7 to 2.2 for craftsmen, production and related workers.

29 This is manifested in a high positive correlation between the frequency of industrial accidents and the proportion of unskilled workers in an industry. The coefficient of correlation for 26 industries in our sample was 0.75, statistically significant at the .01 probability level.

The *location mix* of an industry is considered an important determinant of inter-industry wage differentials for workers of equal skill because of established regional wage differences. Wages are generally higher in Ontario and British Columbia than in Quebec and the Atlantic provinces.

Table 9 shows percentage differentials in wage rates for unskilled labour and maintenance mechanics between Quebec and Ontario in 1970. The table shows that in most industries wage rates for both the unskilled labour and skilled mechanics were higher in Ontario than in Quebec — the notable exceptions were industries like breweries, pulp and paper, tobacco, metal stamping, pharmaceuticals, motor vehicles and petroleum refineries which paid nearly the same wage to their workers in Ontario and Quebec.[30] In general, wage differentials between the two provinces were larger for unskilled workers than for skilled maintenance mechanics.

The figures in Table 9 suggest that if an industry were located in Ontario it would be paying a higher wage than the industry operating in Quebec. Assuming that the regional differences in wage rates were uniform to all occupations, and stable over time,[31] a location mix index could be calculated for each industry from the total proportion of its labour force in each occupational category. The index will, in fact, represent "expected" wage in an industry for a specified occupation, based on historical differentials in wage rates between regions. Since data are not available for either the occupational distribution of employment in each industry by region or for occupational wage rates in each province, a compromise has to be made in estimating location mix. The location mix in this study is represented by "expected" average hourly earnings in each industry based on the proportion of total production employment of an industry in each province of Canada and the provincial average of gross hourly earnings in the manufacturing sector. The computation can be represented by the following formula:

$$LM_i = \frac{\Sigma\ E_{ij} \cdot W_j}{E_i}$$

30 All these industries, except for pharmaceuticals and metal stamping were highly unionized.

31 See Sylvia Ostry and Mahmood A. Zaidi, *Labour Economics in Canada* (Toronto: Macmillan, 1972), pp. 317-336. Ostry and Zaidi show that the wage ranking of provinces was uniform to all occupations and stable since 1939.

where E_{ij} is employment (total manhours, instead of number of employees, were used because of differences in hours worked between regions and industries) of industry i in province j; W_j is the level of average manufacturing hourly earnings in province j, and E_i is total employment in industry i. LM_i is the expected average hourly earnings in industry i based on its regional employment mix.

Table 9

Differentials in Wage Rates Between Ontario and Quebec, 1970

Industry	Unskilled labour			Maintenance mechanics		
	Ontario wage	Quebec wage	Per cent differ-ential	Ontario wage	Quebec wage	Per cent differ-ential
Meat packing	3.04	2.68	13.4	3.66	3.21	14.0
Dairy factories	2.55	2.02	26.2	3.29	2.55	2.9‡
Biscuits	2.92	2.40	21.7	3.80	3.46	9.8
Bakeries	2.76	1.71	61.4	3.58	3.07	16.6
Breweries	4.28	4.16	2.9*	4.70	4.52	4.0
Tobacco	3.35	3.49	−4.2	4.78	4.62	3.5
Rubber	2.94	2.39	23.0	3.70	2.98	25.8
Veneer & plywood mills	2.34	1.75	33.7	3.06	2.63	16.3
Furniture	2.23	1.79	24.6	2.96	2.59	14.3
Pulp and paper	3.09	3.07	0.6	4.35	3.77	15.4
Paper boxes & bags	2.55	2.40	6.2	3.40	3.17	7.2
Iron & steel	3.23	2.80	15.4	4.29	3.73	15.0
Iron foundries	2.93	2.26	29.6	3.42	2.26	17.9
Metal stamping	2.59	2.57	0.8	3.71	3.89	−4.6
Machine shops	2.49	2.13	16.9	3.54	2.76	28.3
Agricultural implements	3.08	1.84	67.4	n.a.	n.a.	—
Aircrafts & parts	3.29	2.51	31.1	4.18	3.61	15.8
Motor vehicles	3.24	3.03	6.9†	4.94	4.67	5.8
Motor vehicle parts	3.37	2.66	26.7*	n.a.	n.a.	—
Industrial electric equipment	2.71	2.37	14.3	3.57	2.99	19.4
Petroleum refineries	3.29	3.33	−1.2	4.49	4.33	3.7
Pharmaceuticals	2.46	2.50	−1.6	3.26	3.29	−0.9
Industrial chemicals	3.12	2.92	6.8	4.09	3.20	27.8

* 1971 rates   † 1969 rates.   ‡ 1968 rates.

Source: *Wage Rates, Salaries and Hours of Labour* (Ottawa: Labour Canada, 1970).

The use of average hourly earnings in the calculation of location mix should not make a significant difference because, as shown in Chapter 2 of this study, the average hourly earnings in an industry are highly correlated with the wage rates for unskilled labour and maintenance mechanics.

The Degree of Unionization The union variable represents the percentage of production workers covered by union agreements in establishments employing more than 20 employees. This approximation to the degree of unionization, necessitated by the lack of data on the number of union members in each industry, may have some bias in favour of industries with large establishments. It may also overestimate the extent of unionization since the employees covered under collective agreements may also include some non-union workers. These biases, however, are not considered very significant bacause, first, industries where there are many small establishments, e.g., machine shops and furniture, are industries with a low degree of unionization, and, secondly, in large manufacturing industries, employing 500 or more workers, 97 per cent of the collective agreements, covering 98 per cent of employees, have a "check-off" provision, and 70 per cent have some kind of union shop.[32]

It should be noted that the specified union variable represents the degree of unionization of all production workers in an industry rather than of workers in individual occupations. The use of this variable in the estimating of the union/non-union wage differential for specific occupations does not present any serious problem because workers in manufacturing industries are generally organized on the basis of their industrial affiliation rather than on craft lines.

The Proportion of the Labour Force in Large Firms Since there are no employment data available for large firms, this study uses the proportion of total value of manufacturing shipments accounted for by the four largest firms in an industry in 1965 (commonly known as "concentration ratio"). The approximation is based on the assumption that the employment in large firms is proportional to their physical output.

The sources of data are given in Appendix B.

---

32 *Provisions in Major Collective Agreements in Canadian Manufacturing Industries, 1969* (Ottawa: Canada Department of Labour). The "check-off" provision relates to committing the employer to deduct from the pay of an employee the amount of union dues and assessments. The "union shop" provision makes membership in the union obligatory as a condition subsequent to continued employment in the plant.

Empirical Results and Their Interpretation

The following empirical form of equation (20) is tested by OLS for explaining the differentials in wage rates of unskilled labourers:

$$(23) \quad \ln W_{ui} = \alpha_0 + \alpha_1 \ln SE_i + \alpha_2 \ln CY_i + \alpha_3 \ln IA_i + \alpha_4 \ln F_i + \alpha_5 \ln RM_i + \alpha_6 U_i C_i$$

where: SE = Seasonality index
IA = Standardized industrial accidents variable
F = Percentage of female production workers
CY = Cyclical variability index
RM = Regional employment mix variable
U = Percentage of workers covered by union agreement
C = Industry concentration ratio (in percentage)
i refers to number of industries 1-26.

All variables, except UC, are in log form. We expect that α_1, α_2, α_3, α_5 and α_6 will be a positive and α_4 will be negative.

The alternative models for unskilled labour in equations (17) and (19) are also tested by replacing U_iC_i by U_i and C_i separately, and by adding the term U_i in equation (23). We expect equation (23) to fit as well or better than the empirical version of alternatives outlined in equations (17), (19) and (21).

For skilled mechanics our expectation is that the following empirical form of equation (21) will work as well or better than equation (23) and the testable form of equation (17) and (19).

$$(24) \quad \ln W_{si} = \beta_0 + \beta_1 \ln SE_i + \beta_2 \ln CY_i + \beta_3 \ln IA_i + \beta_4 \ln F_i + \beta_5 \ln RM_i + \beta_6 C_i$$

It is postulated that β_1, β_2, β_3, β_5 and β_6 are positive and β_4 is negative. The alternatives involve replacing (24) by (23) for skilled workers, and adding the variable U_i in (24).

The results estimated by OLS for unskilled workers are shown in Table 10. Table 11 shows the results for skilled maintenance mechanics.

Estimates of Unskilled Labour Wage Equations by Ordinary Least Squares Regression

Equation number	Dependent variable	Coefficients of regression (T-value in parenthesis)									$\overline{R}^2$	S.E.E.
		Constant	lnSE	lnCY	lnIA	lnF	lnRM	U	C	U.C		
					Estimates of equation (23)							
1.0	$\ln W_u$	1.30	−0.004	−0.013	−0.124	−0.039	−0.089	—	—	0.00004	0.751	0.073
		(2.39)*	(-0.11)	(-1.04)	(-2.99)*	(-4.10)*	(-0.20)			(5.91)*		
					Estimates of alternatives to equation (23)							
1.1	$\ln W_u$	1.60	−0.007	−0.008	−0.151	−0.042	−0.356	0.003	—	—	0.626	0.089
		(2.42)*	(-0.15)	(-0.49)	(-3.04)*	(-3.64)*	(-0.64)	(4.11)*				
1.2	$\ln W_u$	1.55	−0.003	−0.008	−0.141	−0.040	−0.396	0.002	0.002	—	0.773	0.069
		(3.00)*	(-0.07)	(-0.67)	(-3.62)*	(-4.42)*	(0.91)	(3.08)*	(3.65)*			
1.3	$\ln W_u$	1.60	−0.001	−0.007	−0.144	−0.040	−0.456	0.003	0.003	−0.000008	0.761	0.071
		(2.82)*	(-0.04)	(-0.55)	(-3.43)*	(-4.29)*	(-0.91)	(1.66)	(1.36)	(-0.25)		
1.4	$\ln W_u$	1.55	0.016	−0.011	−0.127	−0.044	−0.359	—	0.003	—	0.672	0.084
		(2.49)*	(0.39)	(-0.74)	(-2.73)*	(-4.09)*	(-0.68)		(4.69)*			
1.5	$\ln W_u$	1.35	−0.008	−0.012	−0.128	−0.038	−0.147	0.001	—	0.00003	0.750	0.073
		(2.46)*	(-0.21)	(-0.91)	(-3.11)*	(-4.04)*	(-0.32)	(0.94)		(3.23)*		
1.6	$\ln W_u$	1.31	−0.003	−0.013	−0.121	−0.039	−0.103	—	0.0002	0.00003	0.738	0.075
		(2.31)*	(-0.08)	(-1.00)	(-2.91)*	(-4.00)*	(-0.21)		(0.12)	(2.39)*		
					Non-pecuniary factors only							
1.7	$\ln W_u$	1.64	0.026	−0.013	−0.132	−0.051	−0.256	—	—	—	0.328	0.120
		(1.84)	(0.44)	(-0.59)	(-1.98)	(-3.39)*	(-0.34)					

* Statistically significant at the .05 probability level.

Table 11

Estimates of Skilled Maintenance Mechanics Wage Equations by Ordinary Least Squares Regression

Equation number	Dependent variable	Coefficients of regression (T-value in parenthesis)									$\bar{R}^2$	S.E.E.
		Constant	lnSE	lnCY	lnIA	lnF	lnRM	U	C	U.C		
					Estimates of equation (24)							
2.0	lnW_s	1.82 (3.10)*	0.031 (0.82)	0.001 (0.08)	−0.137 (-3.15)*	−0.025 (-2.47)*	−0.384 (-0.78)	—	0.003 (4.34)*	—	0.600	0.078
					Estimates of alternatives to equation (24)							
2.1	lnW_s	1.88 (2.47)*	0.023 (0.46)	−0.002 (0.12)	−0.152 (-2.66)*	−0.027 (-2.02)	−0.345 (-0.54)	0.002 (1.83)	—	—	0.323	0.102
2.2	lnW_s	1.82 (3.05)*	0.028 (0.70)	−0.002 (0.12)	−0.140 (-3.12)*	−0.024 (-2.33)*	−0.391 (-0.78)	0.0004 (0.47)	0.003 (3.58)*	—	0.583	0.080
2.3	lnW_s	2.17 (3.55)*	0.036 (0.94)	0.008 (0.56)	−0.163 (-3.61)*	−0.027 (-2.67)*	−0.805 (-1.48)	0.003 (1.67)	0.006 (2.72)*	−0.00005 (-1.63)	0.619	0.077
2.4	lnW_s	1.66 (2.53)*	0.019 (0.45)	−0.001 (-0.05)	−0.134 (-2.76)*	−0.023 (-2.00)	−0.180 (-0.33)	—	—	0.00002 (3.37)*	0.501	0.088
2.5	lnW_s	1.63 (2.42)*	0.022 (0.50)	−0.002 (-0.12)	−0.129 (2.56)*	−0.023 (-1.99)	−0.139 (-0.24)	−0.007 (-0.56)	—	0.00003 (2.62)*	0.482	0.089
2.6	lnW_s	1.85 (3.05)*	0.034 (0.85)	0.002 (0.10)	−0.138 (-3.09)*	−0.026 (-2.43)*	−0.422 (-0.82)	—	0.003 (2.14)*	−0.000005 (-0.33)	0.580	0.080
					Non-pecuniary factors only							
2.7	lnW_s	1.89 (2.36)*	0.040 (0.76)	−0.0003 (-0.018)	−0.142 (-2.36)*	−0.031 (-2.29)*	−0.294 (-0.436)	—	—	—	0.244	0.108

Overall Results

The overall results for both unskilled labour and skilled mechanics support our *a priori* expectations. They show that both the institutional variables and the non-institutional variables (or non-pecuniary attributes of employment) are important for explaining the inter-industry differentials in wage rates for workers of equal skill: neither of the two groups of variables, taken separately, is capable of fully accounting for differentials in wage rates of either unskilled labourers or skilled maintenance mechanics. The two sets of variables together explain three-fourths of the total variations in unskilled labour wage rates, and three-fifths of the inter-industry differentials in wage rates of maintenance mechanics. The results support the desirability of an integrated competitive-institutional relative wage determination model for explaining the inter-industry differentials in wage rates for workers of similar skill.

Non-Pecuniary Aspects of Employment

Our results indicate that the five non-pecuniary characteristics of employment are able to explain nearly one-third of the variations in wage rates of unskilled labourers (equation 1.7 in Table 10), and nearly one fourth of the differentials in wage rates of maintenance mechanics (equation 2.7 in Table 11). However, only two — arduousness of work and physical hazard — of the five non-pecuniary factors studied have a significant influence on differentials in wage rates between industries: the seasonality, cyclical instability and the regional mix of employment have no statistically significant effect on the determination of relative wage rates of unskilled labourers and skilled mechanics. Furthermore, whereas the differences in arduousness of work, measured by a proxy of the proportion of females in each industry, have a compensating effect on wage differentials, the differences in the frequency of industrial accidents, an index of differences in physical hazards of employment, are complementary to the differences in relative wage rates of both the unskilled labourers and maintenance mechanics.

Arduousness of Work The coefficient of the proportion of females, approximating the influence of differences in arduousness of work, in the unskilled labourers wage equation in Table 10, and in the maintenance mechanics wage equation in Table 11, indicates that wage rates for unskilled labourers are 5 per cent higher, and for skilled mechanics 3 per cent higher to compensate for a one per cent difference in the proportion of female workers among industries. The elasticities of the unskilled labourers' wage and the maintenance mechanics' wage with respect to onerousness of work are —5 and —3 respectively.[33]

The difference in the wage elasticities of arduousness of work between unskilled labour and maintenance mechanics is due to the nature of their work: the unskilled worker, being a general helper, is affected by the arduousness of work more than the maintenance mechanic who is a skilled technician.

Physical Hazards in Work On *a priori* grounds differences in physical hazards of employment should compensate for inter-industry wage differentials, i.e., an industry where industrial accidents, a measure of physical hazard, occur more often would pay more to its workers. The results of our investigation, indicate that the frequency of industrial accidents is less in high wage industries than in low wage industries. The finding is not peculiar to Canadian industries; the inverse association between the frequency of industrial accidents and wage rates for workers of similar skill has also been found in studies of inter-industry wage differentials in the United States.[34] It may be possible to rationalize this association on the grounds that high relative wage industries have a better industrial safety programme than the low relative wage industries. The inverse relationship between the frequency of industrial accidents and inter-industry wage differentials for skilled and unskilled workers may simply be a statistical association, reflecting the differential impact of industrial safety and the workmen's compensation programme, rather than a causal relationship. The unexpected results may also be a consequence of measurement and aggregation errors in the industrial accidents data.

In the *Wealth of Nations*, the notion of physical hazard as a compensating non-pecuniary factor in wage differentials relates to the differentials between the wage rates of skilled and unskilled workers, and not to the differentials between industries in wage rates of workers of similar skills. We estimated the relationship between skill differentials and the frequency of industrial accidents in our sample of 26 industries and found that it supports the hypothesis. The linear regression of the ratio of unskilled labourers' wage to the wage rate of maintenance mechanics in 26 industries on the frequency of industrial accidents revealed that the

---

33 The coefficient of the proportion of females multiplied by 100 (because the variable has been specified in percentage terms) gives the wage elasticities with respect to onerousness of work.

34 See Mark Lutz, *Equilibrium Wage Structure*.

differences in the frequency of industrial accidents compensate for the differences in wage rates of mechanics and unskilled labourers within industries.[35] The results showed that the percentage spread in wage rates of unskilled labourers and skilled mechanics was lower in industries where the frequency of industrial accidents was higher. The finding supports Adam Smith's proposition with regard to the compensating effect of differences in the physical hazard of employment. The effect of this non-pecuniary factor, as our results indicate, cannot be extended to inter-industry differentials in wage rates for a homogeneous grade of labour.

Irregularity in Employment The results in Tables 10 and 11 disclose that the differences in neither the seasonality nor the cyclical instability of employment have any statistically significant influence on inter-industry differences in wage rates of unskilled workers and maintenance mechanics. The coefficients of seasonality and cyclical instability variables are insignificant in both the unskilled labour wage equation and the maintenance mechanics' wage equation. The results suggest that workers do not appear to consider the regularity or the irregularity of employment in their choice of industries. This attitude may have been shaped by the comprehensive Canadian public unemployment insurance programme and by the union-negotiated supplementary unemployment benefit plans which together largely compensate for the loss of earnings due to seasonality and short term layoffs.

Location Mix It was argued that industries in Ontario and British Columbia, where wage rates are historically higher than the other provinces, pay higher wage rates to workers of similar skill than the industries operating in other parts of Canada. Our results indicate that this is not true of differentials in wage rates of unskilled labourers and maintenance mechanics in the sample of 26 manufacturing industries. Tables 10 and 11 show that the coefficient of regional employment mix in both the unskilled labour and the skilled mechanics' wage equations is statistically insignificant and negative, contrary to the *a priori* expectations

35 The estimate of the relationship is as follows:

$$SD_i = \underset{(32.99)^*}{68.15} + \underset{(3.34)^*}{0.0088\, IAA_i} \qquad \bar{R}^2 = 0.288$$

Where $SD_i = W_{ui}/W_{si}$, the ratio of unskilled labour wage and skilled mechanics wage in i^{th} industry and IAA_i is the frequency of industrial accidents (the difference between IAA_i and IA_i, used in unskilled labour wage equation, is that while IA_i is weighted by the proportion of unskilled workers in an industry, IAA_i is not). * Denotes the significance of the coefficient at the .05 probability level.

towards a positive relationship between wage rates and regional location mix of industries.

The results are not entirely surprising in view of our examination of differentials in wage rates of unskilled labour and maintenance mechanics between Ontario and Quebec (see Table 9). The analysis had indicated that the regional wage differentials for workers of equal skill were significant in some industries and not in others. Some economists have pointed out that unions, among other factors, may be responsible for "equal pay for equal work" in some industries, i.e., highly unionized industries with a national market may disregard the traditional geographical wage differentials and pay the same wage scale wherever their plants are located.[36] The hypothesis is supported by the figures in Table 9 which show that highly unionized industries such as breweries, tobacco, pulp and paper, motor vehicles assembly and industrial chemicals pay almost the same wage rate to unskilled workers and maintenance mechanics in Ontario and Quebec. To further test this hypothesis the sample of 26 industries was divided into two, one where 85 or more per cent of the workers were covered by a union agreement, and the other where the percentage of unionized workers in the total workforce was less than 85 per cent. Wage rates of unskilled labourers and of maintenance mechanics in each of the two samples were regressed against the five non-pecuniary attributes of employment, including the regional employment mix. The estimates of the regression are shown in Table 12.

The results disclose that the coefficient of regional employment mix is positive and statistically significant in the sample of industries where less than 85 per cent of workers are unionized. On the other hand, in the group of highly unionized industries (where more than 85 per cent of workers are unionized) the coefficient of regional employment mix is negative and statistically significant. The results suggest that in industries where unionization is less than 85 per cent of the total workforce, geographic wage differentials affect the inter-industry wage differentials, i.e., if an industry is located in a high wage province it pays more than the industry located in a low wage province to workers of similar skills. The geographic wage premium for both unskilled workers and skilled maintenance mechanics in these industries is almost the same as indicated by nearly similar coefficients in unskilled labour and mechanics wage regressions. The regional employment mix appears to have the opposite effect on wage rates in the group of highly unionized industries, i.e., highly unionized industries appear to pay less to work-

36 See Richard A. Lester, *Economics of Labor*, 2nd ed. (New York: Macmillan, 1964), pp. 314-315.

Table 12

Relationship Between Wage Rates and Regional Employment Mix in Highly Unionized and Low Unionized Industries: Regression Results

Model: $\ln W_i = \alpha + \alpha_1 \ln SE_i + \alpha_2 \ln CY_i + \alpha_3 \ln IA_i + \alpha_4 \ln F_i + \alpha_5 \ln RM_i$

Industry characteristics	Highly unionized industries (U > 85%)		Low unionized industries (U < 85%)	
	Unskilled labour	Maintenance mechanics	Unskilled labour	Maintenance mechanics
Constant	3.08 (5.83)*	3.17 (4.87)*	−2.65 (-2.50)*	−1.99 (-1.61)
Seasonality	0.058 (1.44)	0.077 (1.54)	0.077 (1.52)	0.094 (1.58)
Regional mix	−1.33 (-3.61)*	−1.34 (-2.95)*	3.67 (3.72)*	3.39 (2.95)*
Frequency of industrial accidents	−0.200 (-3.91)*	−0.192 (-3.04)*	−0.126 (-2.38)*	−0.167 (-2.72)
Proportion of females	−0.028 (-3.03)*	−0.008 (-0.67)	−0.41 (-2.86)*	−0.033 (-1.99)
Cyclical variability	−0.019 (-1.35)	−0.003 (-0.17)	−0.073 (-3.39)*	−0.051 (-2.02)
Dependent variable	$\ln W_u$	$\ln W_s$	$\ln W_u$	$\ln W_s$
S.E.E.	0.048	0.059	0.074	0.086
$\bar{R}^2$	0.822	0.637	0.675	0.528
Number of observations	13	13	13	13

* Significant at the .05 probability level.

Note: W_u and W_s refer to wage rates of unskilled labour and maintenance mechanics respectively.

ers of equal skill in high wage regions than in low wage regions. This finding is puzzling and contrary to *a priori* expectations.

Institutional Variables

The results in Tables 10 and 11 are quite consistent with the institutional theory formulated in equations (23) and (24). It seems likely on the basis of these results that unions have no influence on relative wage rates for skilled workers, but that they are able to obtain a wage premium for unskilled workers by insisting upon equitable differentials between wage rates of skilled and unskilled labour. The competing hypothesis, which maintains, without a sound theoretical rationale, that both unions and large firm concentration in the product market have independent influence on relative wage rates for a homogeneous grade of labour in different industries, does not perform quite as well in the case of skilled labour. For unskilled labour the competing hypothesis does no better than the theory estimated by equation (23).

Skilled Labour The equations (2.1) to (2.6) in Table 11 show that unions have no effect on relative wage rates for skilled maintenance mechanics. The mechanics' wages are, however, 30 per cent higher in a totally concentrated industry — where four firms account for the total industry output — than in a perfectly competitive industry (equation 2.0 in Table 11).[37] Differences in the degree of large firm concentration in industry product markets explain nearly one-third of the differentials in wage rates of skilled maintenance mechanics in 26 Canadian manufacturing industries.

The competing model of equation (17), whose estimates are given in equations (2.1) and (2.2) in Table 11, does not fare well: first, the predictive power of the model is less than the model of equation (24), and secondly, the coefficient of unionization has no significance either individually or with the concentration variable. The empirical form of the second alternative model of equation (19), which includes U_i, C_i and the interaction term U_iC_i on the grounds that union-nonunion wage differentials are linearly dependent on the degree of concentration in the product market, also does not perform quite as well as equation (24);

37 To calculate the relative wage effects of unionization and large firm concentration from Tables 10 and 11, the coefficients should be multiplied by 100 because the variables U_i and C_i have been specified in percentage terms. The interpretation of the coefficients of $U_i.C_i$ term requires multiplying the coefficient by 10,000 since the maximum value of $U_i.C_i$ is 10,000 when U_i and C_i are both 100 per cent.

although the predictive power of this model is slightly higher than our model in equation (24), the two variables, U_i and U_iC_i, that distinguish it from our model, are not statistically significant (see equation 2.3 in Table 11). Similarly, the institutional model (outlined for unskilled labour) of equation (23) also does not fare as well for skilled mechanics as the model of equation (24). The empirical results of this model are shown in equation (2.4) in Table 11. They show that although the coefficient of the interaction variable UC is statistically significant, the predictive power of the model is rather less than of our model. The model of equation (24), therefore, appears to be the best theoretically sound explanation of differentials in wage rates of skilled workers in Canadian industries.

Unskilled Labour Equation (1.0) in Table 10, the fitted version of equation (23), shows that the union policy of equitable internal wage differentials leads to a 40 per cent higher wage rate for unskilled labour in completely concentrated fully unionized industries than in perfectly competitive totally non-unionized industries. The institutional theory of equitable internal wage differentials, tested by equation (23), explains 75 per cent of the differentials in wage rates of unskilled labourers in 26 Canadian manufacturing industries: 40 per cent of the differentials are explained by the interaction variable alone. The theory does as well as the competing models of wage determination for unskilled labour.

The alternative model of equation (17), which predicts an independent union and large firm influence on relative wage rates, does have a slightly better predictive power than the model outlined in equation (23). The results of this model are shown by the estimates of equation (1.2) in Table 10. The coefficient of unionization in equation (1.2) suggests that if an industry is completely unionized it pays a 20 per cent higher wage rate to unskilled workers than the non-unionized industry. Similarly the coefficient of concentration ratio indicates that oligopolistic industries, where a few large firms account for total industry output, pay a 20 per cent higher wage than the competitive industries. In view of the lack of theoretical rationale for either coefficient, it seems possible that both coefficients may be representing the same force that is captured by UC in our formulation of equation (23). This idea receives support from the fact that when we introduce the interaction term in this model (see equation 1.3 in Table 10), the coefficients of all institutional variables become statistically insignificant.

The model in equation (24), postulated for skilled labour, does not work as well for unskilled labour as equation (23): its predictive power (see equation 1.4 in Table 10) is rather less than the explanatory strength of equation (23). Moreover, the significant coefficient of concentration ratio cannot be defended on theoretical grounds: there seems to be no rationale for an independent wage premium to unskilled workers in large firms since the cost of hiring and training of unskilled labour is considered negligible.

The model of equation (23) should therefore be regarded as the best of the suggested possible explanations for inter-industry differentials in wage rates for unskilled workers, partly because it does as well as other alternative models, but mainly because it can be defended on theoretical grounds.

The results of our model imply that a union's ability to obtain a wage premium for unskilled labour depends on the structure of the product market. If the product market is fully competitive (means that $C_i = 0$, and therefore $U_iC_i = 0$) unionized workers do not get any wage premium and wage rates are determined purely by the market forces: the differentials in wage rates are attributed solely to the inter-industry differences in non-pecuniary attributes of employment. On the other hand, if the product market of an industry is purely oligopolistic ($C_i = 100\%$) — there are only four large firms in an industry — and all workers in the industry are unionized ($U_i = 100\%$), then unskilled workers in that industry receive a 40 per cent higher wage rate than the wage rate in fully competitive non-unionized industries. The rationale for this wage premium is that skilled workers receive a wage premium in fully oligopolistic industries independently of unionization, and the industrial unions are able to get a higher wage rate for their members in an unskilled occupational category by insisting upon equitable wage differentials between unskilled and skilled workers. Table 13 below shows the union-nonunion wage differential for unskilled labour under varying degrees of large firm concentration in the product market and of unionization.

The table suggests that the percentage wage impact of unionization increases proportionately with the increase in the proportion of total output (or total employment) accounted for by large firms. For example if four large firms account for only 10 percent of the output in industry A and 50 per cent of the output in industry B, and if all workers in the two industries are unionized, unskilled workers get only a 4 per cent wage premium over the competitive wage in industry A and 20 per cent in industry B. Thus, unions affect wage rates of unskilled workers because of oligopolistic control of the product market.

Some Ancillary Evidence The institutional theory relating to the union policy of equitable wage differentials is also supported by the high positive correlation between wage rates of skilled mechanics and unskilled workers in our sample of 26 industries, and by the positive relation-

Table 13

Percentage Wage Premium (Over the Competitive Wage) for Unskilled Workers Under Varying Degree of Unionism (U_i) and Degree of Large Firm Concentration (C_i)

Value of U_i (in percentages)	Value of C_i (in percentage)			
	10	20	50	100
10	0.4	0.8	2	4
20	0.8	1.6	4	8
50	2	4	10	20
100	4	8	20	40

Source: Equation (1.0) in Table 10.

ship between the degree of unionization and the percentage spread in wage rates of unskilled and skilled labour. The high positive correlation in two occupational wage rates indicates that wage rates for unskilled labour are high in industries where skilled labour wage rates are high[38] (our results show that wage rates of skilled labour are higher in concentrated industries than in competitive industries). The positive relationship between percentage spread in two occupational wage rates and the degree of unionization, estimated by an Ordinary Least Squares regression, suggests that, because of the union policy of equitable internal wage differentials, the skill differentials are lower in unionized indus-

38 The correlation between wage rates of unskilled labourers and skilled maintenance mechanics in 26 industries yielded a coefficient of 0.86, statistically significant at the .01 probability level. A linear regression between the two wage rates indicated that a one per cent change in skilled labour wage rates leads to a nearly one per cent change in wage rates of unskilled labour. The estimate of this regression is as follows:

$$\ln W_{ui} = \underset{(-2.61)^*}{-0.32} + \underset{(8.56)^*}{1.02 \ln W} \qquad \overline{R}^2 = 0.774;\ \text{S.E.E.} = 0.074$$

where W_{ui} and W_{si} are wage rates of unskilled labourers and skilled mechanics respectively. * Denotes significance of the coefficients at the .05 probability level.

tries than in non-unionized industries. Table 14, which gives the results of this regression, shows that the percentage differentials between wage rates of unskilled labourers and maintenance mechanics are 13-18 per cent lower in completely unionized industries than in non-unionized industries (13 per cent when the relationship between skill differentials and unionization is controlled for the differences in onerousness of work and the frequency of industrial accidents, 18 per cent when the influence of these non-institutional variables is not held constant).

Summary of Results

Wage rates for workers of similar skill differ between industries in Canada because of differences in non-pecuniary attributes of employment, degree of unionization and the degree of large firm concentration in the product market of industries. Nearly three-fourths of the differences in wage rates of unskilled labourers are due to non-pecuniary aspects of employment and the union policy of equitable internal wage differentials which tends to raise wage rates of unskilled workers in oligopolistic industries where skilled labour wage rates are higher than in competitive industries. Similarly, nearly three-fifths of the inter-industry differentials in wage rates of skilled mechanics can be attributed to varying degrees of non-pecuniary characteristics of employment and the degree of large firm concentration in the product market of industries. The evidence is consistent with the proposition that unions have no power to cause wage rates of skilled workers to differ by industry. They do appear to cause differentials in wages of unskilled labour among industries, but their influence here depends upon the structure of the product market. Since industries dominated by a few large firms pay a wage premium to skilled workers over the competitive wage for greater selectivity in recruiting and for stable attachment, because of high cost of hiring and training of skilled labour, unions are able to obtain a wage premium for unskilled workers by insisting upon equitable internal wage differentials. This union policy is reflected in their demands for general wage increases for all workers irrespective of their skill level, and results in a lower percentage spread in unionized industries than in non-unionized industries. Thus the wage rates for skilled workers are higher in only those industries where large firms account for a significant proportion of total employment and output, independently of unionization. These industries pay a higher rate to unionized unskilled workers because of union policy of equitable internal wage differentials.

Table 14

Relationship Between the Degree of Unionization and the Skill Differentials Within Industries

Model: $\ln\left(\frac{W_u}{W_s}\right) = \alpha_o + \alpha_1 \ln F_i + \alpha_2 IAA_i + \alpha_3 U_i$

Dependent variable	Equation number	Coefficients of regression (T-value in parenthesis) Constant	lnFi	lnIAAi	Ui	$\bar{R}^2$	S.E.E.
$\ln\left(\frac{W_u}{W_s}\right)$	1.0	−0.69 (-5.84)*	−0.009 (-1.44)	0.049 (2.69)*	0.0013 (2.69)*	0.481	0.052
$\ln\left(\frac{W_u}{W_s}\right)$	1.1	−0.74 (-6.53)*	—	0.053 (2.89)*	0.0014 (3.03)*	0.457	0.053
$\ln\left(\frac{W_u}{W_s}\right)$	1.2	−0.65 (-4.88)*	−0.013 (-1.87)	0.058 (2.91)*	—	0.340	0.059
$\ln\left(\frac{W_u}{W_s}\right)$	1.3	−0.39 (-8.21)*	−0.12 (-1.67)	—	0.0016 (2.90)*	0.340	0.059
$\ln\left(\frac{W_u}{W_s}\right)$	1.4	−0.26 (-13.32)*	−0.018 (-2.21)*	—	—	0.135	0.067
$\ln\left(\frac{W_u}{W_s}\right)$	1.5	−0.72 (-5.44)*	—	0.066 (3.22)*	—	0.272	0.062
$\ln\left(\frac{W_u}{W_s}\right)$	1.6	−0.44 (-10.13)*	—	—	0.0018 (3.35)*	0.290	0.061

* Statistically significant at the .05 probability level.

The five non-pecuniary characteristics of employment specified in this study, namely the onerousness of work, the frequency of industrial accidents, seasonality and the cyclical instability in employment, and the regional location of industries, explain nearly one-third of the inter-industry differentials in wage rates of unskilled labourers and nearly one-fourth of the differentials in wage rates of maintenance mechanics.

The *arduousness of work* is the most significant factor in inter-industry wage differentials for workers of equal skill. A one per cent difference in the proportion of females, a proxy for onerousness of work, appears to cause a 5 per cent compensating wage differential for unskilled labour and a 3 per cent difference in wage rates of maintenance mechanics among industries.

Industries paying a high relative wage to unskilled labour and maintenance mechanics have a lower *frequency of industrial accidents* than other industries. However, in industries where the frequency of industrial accidents is lower than the others, the percentage spread in wage rates of maintenance mechanics and unskilled labourers is higher than in other industries.

The *seasonality and cyclical instability* of employment do not appear to affect differentials in wage rates of either unskilled labour or of maintenance mechanics.

The inter-industry differentials in wage rates of unskilled labour and of maintenance mechanics are not affected by the regional location of industries. Although no firm conclusions can be drawn because of the small sample of industries, the regional location of industries gives rise to compensating wage differentials between industries for both unskilled labour and maintenance mechanics if these industries are not very highly unionized.

Implications The empirical results of this study have at least two important implications for wage theory and research. First, they suggest the necessity of integrating competitive theory and the institutional approach for the explanation of wage differentials. Second, the results outline the need for studying the inter-relationship of internal wage structure within industries and the external wage structure for workers of similar skill between industries for a better understanding of institutional wage mechanisms. This calls for micro studies of wage determination in industries with varying structure of the product market.

4
Summary and Conclusions

This study was undertaken to investigate why some industries in Canada pay higher wages than others to workers of similar skill. The questions we sought to answer were, first, whether differentials in wage rates for similar work persist because of compensating differentials in non-pecuniary characteristics of employment; secondly, whether unionized industries pay a higher wage than non-unionized industries; thirdly, whether wages of all workers or only of skilled workers are higher in oligopolistic industries; and fourthly, whether unions are more effective in increasing relative wage rates in industries dominated by large firms than in competitive industries. The answers to these questions have a significant bearing on the competitive theory of the labour market, which predicts equalization of "net advantages" in the long run and relates the persistent inter-industry wage differentials for a homogeneous grade of labour to the compensating differentials in non-pecuniary attributes of employment among industries. They are also of significance to the institutional theory of relative wage determination, which stresses the power of trade unions and organized management to cause wage differentials for similar work.

The study first analyzed wage rates of unskilled labourers and skilled maintenance mechanics in 26 Canadian manufacturing industries, and discovered that significant inter-industry wage differentials have existed for these two occupations, each of which is homogeneous, since 1952. The study also revealed that wage supplements were related to the level of wage rates, so that similar differentials existed in total monetary rewards.

To explain why wage rates for a homogeneous grade of labour are higher in some industries than others, we developed an integrated relative wage determination model. The model postulated that relative wage rates for workers of similar skill among industries were dependent on the differences in non-pecuniary characteristics of employment, extent of unionization and the degree of large firm concentration in the product market of industries. It was argued that the relative wage influence of unions and large firms would be asymmetric for unskilled and skilled labour: large firms would pay a wage premium to skilled workers, for greater selectivity in recruiting and for stable attachment — the main reason being the higher cost of hiring and training skilled workers in large firms than in small firms. It was hypothesized that trade unions would have no effect on relative wage rates for skilled labour. They, however, could obtain a wage premium for unskilled workers in oligopolistic industries, somewhat similar to the wage premium for skilled labour, by insisting upon equitable internal wage differentials. The model was fitted to the differentials in average wage rates of unskilled labourers and maintenance mechanics in 26 Canadian manufacturing industries.

The empirical evidence, based on the results of ordinary least squares regression, supports the theory outlined in the study: the integrated wage model is able to explain three-fourths of the differentials in wage rates of unskilled labourers, and three-fifths of the variations in wage rates of skilled mechanics in 26 Canadian industries. It seems likely on the basis of our results, that trade unions have no effect on relative wage rates for skilled labour, but that they are able to create wage differentials among industries for unskilled labour by insisting upon equitable internal wage differentials. Our results indicate that wage rates for skilled mechanics are 30 per cent higher in completely oligopolistic industries, where four firms account for the total industry output and employment, than in the purely competitive industries, independent of unionization. Unions, by organizing all workers in an industry, can obtain up to a 40 per cent higher wage for unskilled workers depending upon the degree of large firm concentration in the industry: if an industry is totally oligopolistic and completely unionized, unskilled workers receive a 40 per cent higher wage than the purely competitive non-unionized industries. Unions do not appear to have any influence on relative wage rates for either unskilled or skilled workers in purely competitive industries.

The study reveals that nearly one-third of the inter-industry differentials in wage rates of unskilled labourers, and almost one-quarter of the wage differentials for maintenance mechanics can be attributed to differences in non-pecuniary characteristics of industries. Of the five non-pecuniary factors analyzed in this study, only two — arduousness of work and physical hazard — were found to be of significance to inter-industry wage differentials: the cyclical and seasonal instability of employment, and the regional employment mix do not appear to have any influence on relative wage rates of either unskilled or skilled workers. Differences in arduousness of work — whose influence was measured by a proxy of the proportion of female workers — may lead to a 5 per cent difference in wage rates of unskilled labourers and a 3 per cent difference in wage rates of skilled mechanics among industries. Differences in the frequency of industrial accidents — an index of physical hazard — are inversely related to the differences in wage rates for skilled and unskilled workers. The inverse association is somewhat puzzling and contrary to *a priori* expectations towards a positive relationship between relative wage rates and the severity of physical hazard. Our finding suggests that industries paying a high relative wage to workers of similar skills have a better industrial safety programme than others.

Implications

The empirical findings of this study emphasize the necessity of an integrated theory of relative wage determination, incorporating the basic elements of competitive wage theory and the institutional approach. For a complete understanding of wage relationships and wage institutions, the wage theory should explicitly take account of the non-pecuniary aspects of employment, trade unions and the presence of large firms in the product market. It is also necessary to inter-relate the external wage structure between industries and the internal wage structure within industries. Although this interrelationship, as well as the relationship between the wage structure and the general wage level was emphasized by Dunlop as early as 1954, little progress has been made in this direction.[1] It might be desirable to undertake more micro studies of firms and industries, where it may be possible to examine in depth the relationship between wage rates for varying skills and job characteristics. Such studies of production units with a varying degree of trade union control of the labour market and of large firm concentration in the product market could be invaluable in building a general theory of wage determination.

Because of the limited availability of data this study, like many previous studies of wage differentials, covered only manufacturing industries. While its results can almost certainly be generalized for the manufacturing sector, they may not have validity for the non-manufacturing sector, particularly the service sector where unions are comparatively weak and small firms dominate the market. Since service industries employ more than one half of the total Canadian labour force there is a great need for investigation of the process of wage determination in these industries. Research on this sector has been handicapped by the lack of adequate wage and related data.

---

1 Dunlop, *The Theory of Wage Determination*, pp. 14-15.

In conclusion, it is our hope that this study will contribute to a better understanding of wage setting mechanisms and wage institutions in Canada, an area which has received relatively little attention from students of economics and industrial relations. It is our hope also that it will stimulate further research on this important topic. For, whatever this study may have added to existing knowledge, much remains to be done in this field.

Appendix A

Titles and Standard Classification Number of Industries Surveyed in this Study

Industry name	Classification number
Slaughtering & Meat Processing	101
Dairy Factories	105
Biscuits	128
Bakeries	129
Breweries	145
Tobacco Products	153
Rubber Products	161, 163, 169
Leather Tanneries	172
Veneer & Plywood Mills	252
Household, Office & Other Furniture	261, 264, 266
Pulp & Paper	271
Paper Boxes & Bags	273
Iron & Steel Mills	291
Iron Foundries	294
Metal Stamping, Pressing & Coating	304
Machine Shops	308
Agricultural Implements	311
Office & Store Machinery	318
Aircraft & Parts	321
Motor Vehicles	323
Motor Vehicles Parts and Accessories	325
Small Electrical Appliances	331
Electrical Industrial Equipment	336
Petroleum Refineries	365
Pharmaceuticals, Medicines & Toilet Preparations	374, 377
Industrial Chemicals	378

Source: *Standard Industrial Classification Manual.* Ottawa: Dominion Bureau of Statistics, 1960.

Appendix B

Sources of Data

Wage Data

Canada Department of Labour, *Wage Rates, Salaries and Hours of Labour* (Ottawa: Information Canada, Annual). Wage Rates refer to straight-time average hourly rates. They exclude overtime payments, shift differentials, non-production bonuses, shares in company profits and the monetary value of employee benefits, but include cost-of-living bonus payments. The wage rates are compiled by the Department of Labour from an annual occupational wage survey of industries. The survey covers all establishments employing twenty or more workers in any month of the year.

Seasonality

The monthly data on the number of wage earners were obtained directly from the Labour Division, Statistics Canada, Ottawa.

Cyclical Variability

Statistics Canada, *Indexes of Real Domestic Product by Industry,* Catalogue Numbers 61-506, 61-510 and 61-005 (Ottawa: Information Canada).

Industrial Accidents

U.S. Department of Labor, *Handbook of Labor Statistics,* Bulletin Number 1705 (Washington: U.S. Government Printing Office).

Proportion of Unskilled Labour by Industry

Dominion Bureau of Statistics, *The 1961 Census of Canada,*Volume 3.3, Catalogue Number 94-518 (Ottawa: Queen's Printer,1964).

Proportion of Females and Regional Mix

Statistics Canada, *General Review of the Manufacturing Industries of Canada* (Ottawa: Information Canada, Annual). The data are an average of 1961-1970.

Unionization

Canada Department of Labour, *Working Conditions in Canadian Industry* (Ottawa: Information Canada, Annual). The figures are an average of 1967-1969.

Industry Concentration Ratios

Department of Consumer and Corporate Affairs, *Concentration in the Manufacturing Industries of Canada* (Ottawa: Information Canada, 1971).

Appendix C

Nature and Limitations of Wage Data Used in this Study

The wage data used in this study are based on annual occupational wage survey of industries, conducted by the Canada Department of Labour and published in *Wage Rates, Salaries and Hours of Labour* (Ottawa: Information Canada, Annual). The survey covers all establishments in an industry employing 20 or more workers.

The survey is conducted by means of a reporting form mailed to employers. Among other things the form includes a short description of work characteristics of occupations surveyed. The occupational descriptions of unskilled labourers and maintenance mechanics are as follows:

Labourers (Male, Production Departments) Performs various unskilled light or heavy manual duties in departments engaged directly in production, frequently moving from one duty to another: performs duties such as moving empty, partially filled and filled tote boxes or other containers to and from processing operations, removing waste products to disposal areas, cleaning machinery or equipment in production areas, uses simple tools and equipment in performing duties.

Labourer (Male, Non-Production, Maintenance and Service) Performs various unskilled light or heavy manual duties such as lifting, carrying, moving and stacking materials or equipment, hand-shoveling loose materials, collecting and disposing of refuse; digging and levelling roads and ditches; uses simple tools and equipment in performing duties.

Maintenance Mechanic (Machine Repairman) Maintains and repairs machinery and mechanical equipment; examines machinery to diagnose source of trouble, dismantles machine after locating defect; replaces defective part, obtaining replacement from stock or having part made by machine shop; reassembles machine and makes operating adjustments (does not include automotive repairmen).

The above descriptions contained in the Survey questionnaire are not meant to be exact "standards" for jobs in any industry or establishment. They are designed to help employers identify the specific jobs for which information is sought. For example, although duties of both production department and maintenance labourers are described separately employers are not asked to report wage rates for each of the two departments. Information is sought for establishments rather than for companies.

Nature of Data

The wage data collected by the survey has the following characteristics:

The wage rate does not include overtime payments, shift differentials, non-production bonuses, shares in company profits, and the monetary value of various employee benefits such as group insurance, retirement pensions, health plan premiums, sick benefits, uniforms etc. The rates are derived before deductions are made for taxes, unemployment insurance, pensions, etc. They include cost-of-living bonuses when applicable.

Workers on piece work or other incentive systems are separated from those on straight time rates.

The rates apply to only qualified workers in each reported occupation. Rates for beginners, learners, apprentices, helpers, handicapped workers, part-time workers and other supervisory personnel are not included.

The rates apply to day work only.

Wage rates relate to a "normal" pay period preceding October 1, that is, a period in which there were no strikes, unusual lay-offs or any other abnormal condition.

The reported wage rate is an hourly rate. When daily, weekly or monthly rates are reported employers are asked to report the number of hours worked in a week to facilitate conversion to an hourly rate.

Industry Average The occupational wage rates by establishment are converted into an industry average wage rate for publication. The average is obtained by multiplying establishment wage rates by the number of employees in an occupation; the sum of this product is then divided by the total number of employees in the occupation.

Limitation

The industry average is effected by variations in wage rates for similar jobs between establishments. There is evidence that significant inter-establishment differentials exist in many manufacturing industries in Canada. An analysis of inter-decile range (the middle 80 per cent of the wage distribution) of establishment wage rates of unskilled labourers within ten manufacturing industries in Ontario in 1957 revealed that inter-establishment wage variations ranged from .219 cents an hour in pulp and paper mills to 63.5 cents an hour in sheet metal products industry (metal stamping, pressing and coating industry in the new industrial classification).[1] A similar variation in wage rates between establishments was also found in Quebec. The analysis also disclosed that the wage dispersion between establishments was greater than the inter-industry wage differentials for unskilled labourers.

Some analysts have raised doubts about the use of industry aggregates in the study of wage structure on the grounds that inter-industry wage differentials may not give the true picture of differentials in wage rates for similar jobs. We, however, feel that the study of both inter-industry wage differentials and inter-establishment differentials are desirable, and in some sense complementary. Research on wage variations within establishments in a given industry is necessary to fully understand the process of wage determination at the industry level, particularly for a better understanding of the relationship between wage rates and job and personal characteristics of workers. This research has been hampered by a total absence of published data on wage rates within industries.

The study of inter-industry wage differentials is equally significant to assess the relative wage impact of industrial unions, industry product market structures and the non-pecuniary aspects of employment among industries.

---

1 Sylvia Ostry, "Inter-Establishment Dispersion of Occupational Wage Rates, Ontario and Quebec, 1957", *Canadian Journal of Economics and Political Science,* 26 (1960): 277-288. The study was based on unpublished wage data and covered 1250 establishment rates for hourly rated male unskilled labourers in the manufacturing industries of Ontario and Quebec. Sample of industries included carbonated beverages, hosiery and knit goods, lumber saw mills, wooden furniture, saw mills, paper boxes, pulp and paper mills, iron foundries, special industrial machinery and sheet metal products.

Bibliography

Readings and Essays

Aronson, Robert, *et al*. *Essays on Industrial Relations Research*. Ann Arbor: Institute of Labor and Industrial Relations, University of Michigan - Wayne State University, 1961.

Burton, John F., *et al*. *Readings in Labor Market Analysis*. New York: Holt, Rinehart and Winston, 1971.

Chamberlain, Neil W., *et al*. *A Decade of Industrial Relations Research, 1946-1956*. New York: Harper, 1966.

Gordon, R. A. and M. Gordon, eds. *Prosperity and Unemployment*. New York: Wiley, 1966.

Hugh-Jones, E. M., ed. *Wage Structure in Theory and Practice*. Amsterdam: North-Holland, 1966.

Hunter, Laurence, ed. *Labour Market Under Different Employment Conditions*. London: Allen and Unwin, 1971.

Industrial Relations Research Association. *A Review of Industrial Relations Research*. Vol. 1. Madison, 1970.

International Economic Association. *The Theory of Wage Determination*. Edited by J. T. Dunlop. London: Macmillan, 1957.

Marshall, Ray and Richard Perlman. *An Anthology of Labor Economics: Readings and Commentary*. New York: Wiley, 1972.

McConnell, Campbell R. *Perspectives on Wage Determination*. New York: McGraw-Hill, 1970.

Meij, J. L., ed. *Internal Wage Structure*. Amsterdam: North-Holland, 1963.

National Bureau of Economic Research. *Aspects of Labor Economics*. Princeton: Princeton University Press, 1962.

Perlman, Richard, ed. *Wage Determination: Market or Power Forces*. Boston: Heath, 1964.

Phelps, Edmund S., *et al*. *Microeconomic Foundations of Employment and Inflation Theory*.New York: Norton, 1970.

Taylor, George W. and Frank C. Pearson. *New Concepts in Wage Determination*. New York: McGraw-Hill, 1957.

Books

Becker, Gary S. *Human Capital: A Theoretical and Empirical Analysis With Special Reference to Education*. New York: National Bureau of Economic Research, 1964.

———. *Economic Theory*. New York: Knopf, 1971.

Cartter, Allan M. *Theory of Wages and Employment.* Homewood: Richard D. Irwin, 1959.

Coombs, Whitney. *The Wages of Unskilled Labor in Manufacturing Industries in the United States, 1890-1924.* New York: Columbia University Press, 1926.

Corina, John. *Labour Market Economics: A Short Survey of Recent Theory.* London: Heinemann, 1972.

Finkel, Sidney R. and Vincent J. Tarascio. *Wage and Employment Theory.* New York: Ronald Press, 1971.

Fisher, Malcom R. *The Economic Analysis of Labour.* London: Weidenfeld and Nicolson, 1971.

Fleisher, Belton, M. *Labor Economics: Theory and Evidence.* Englewood Cliffs: Prentice-Hall, 1970.

Friedman, Milton. *Price Theory: A Provisional Text.* Chicago: Aldine, 1962.

Glasser, C. *Wage Differentials: The Case of the Unskilled.* New York: Columbia University Press, 1940.

Hicks, J. R. *The Theory of Wages.* London: Macmillan, 1963.

Lewis, H. G. *Unionism and Relative Wages in the United States.* Chicago: University of Chicago Press, 1963.

Lester, Richard A. *Economics of Labor.* 2nd ed. New York: Macmillan, 1964.

Marshall, Alfred. *Principles of Economics.* 8th ed. London: Macmillan, 1962.

Organisation for Economic Cooperation and Development. *Wages and Labour Mobility.* Paris: O.E.C.D., 1965.

Ostry, Sylvia and Mahmood A. Zaidi. *Labour Economics in Canada.* 2nd ed. Toronto: Macmillan, 1972.

Perlman, Richard. *Labor Theory.* New York: Wiley, 1969.

Porter, Allan A., *et al. Wages in Canada and the United States.* Occasional Paper No. 6, Canada Department of Labour. Ottawa: Queen's Printer, 1969.

Rees, Albert. *The Economics of Trade Unions.* Chicago: University of Chicago Press, 1962.

———. *The Economics of Work and Pay.* New York: Harper, 1973.

Reynolds, Lloyd G. *The Structure of Labor Markets.* New York: Harper, 1951.

Reynolds, Lloyd G. and Cynthia H. Taft. *The Evolution of Wage Structure.* New Haven: Yale University Press, 1956.

Salkever, L. R. *Wage Structure Theory.* New York: Humanities Press, 1964.

Saunders, George. *Wage Determination in Canada.* Occasional Paper No.

3, Canada Department of Labour. Ottawa: Queen's Printers, 1965.

Smith, Adam. *The Wealth of Nations.* Edited by Edwin Cannan. Vol. I. Strand: Methuen, 1961.

Steiber, Jack. *The Steel Industry Wage Structure.* Cambridge: Harvard University Press, 1959.

Articles

Ashenfelter, Orley and George E. Johnson. "Unionism, Relative Wages and Labor Quality in U.S. Manufacturing Industries." *International Economic Review* 13 (October, 1972): 488-508.

Bailey, William R., *et al.* "Wage Differentials and Establishment Size, Union Status and Industry Concentration." *American Statistical Association Proceedings,* 1970, pp. 395-401.

Behman, Sara. "Wage Determining Process in U.S. Manufacturing." *Quarterly Journal of Economics* 76 (February, 1968): 117-42.

————. "Labour Mobility, Increasing Labour Demand and Money Wage Rate Increases in the United States Manufacturing." *Review of Economic Studies* 11 (October, 1964): 253-66.

Basett, Lowell, R. and Thomas E. Borcherding. "The Firm, the Industry and the Long-Run Demand for Factors of Production." *Canadian Journal of Economics* 3 (February, 1970): 140-46.

Brechling, Frank. "Wage Inflation and the Structure of Regional Unemployment." *Journal of Money, Credit and Banking* 5, Part 2 (February, 1973): 355-84.

Brosnan, Peter. "Predicting Workers' Preferences." *British Journal of Industrial Relations* 11 (July, 1973): 291-96.

Else, P. K. "The Demand for Factors of Production : A Graphical Analysis." *Bulletin of Economic Research* 23 (1971): 24-34.

Gallaway, L. E. "Labour Mobility, Resource Allocation and Structural Unemployment." *American Economic Review* 53 (September, 1963): 694-716.

Hicks, J. R. "Economic Foundations of Wage Policy." *Economic Journal* 65 (September, 1955): 389-404.

Johnson, G. E. "Wage Theory and Inter-Regional Variation." *Industrial Relations* 6 (May, 1967): 321-38.

Leigh, Duane, E. "An Empirical Investigation of the Determinants of the Level of Unemployment in Six Major Occupations." *Western Economic Journal* 10 (December, 1972): 384-95.

Maurice, S. Charles. "Long-Run Factor Demand in a Perfectly Competitive Economy." *Journal of Political Economy* 80 (November-December, 1972): 1271-79.

McGuire, T. W. and L. A. Rapping. "Interindustry Wage Change Dispersion and the "Spillover" Hypothesis." *American Economic Review* 56 (June, 1966): 493-501.

———. "The Role of Market Variables and Key Bargains in the Manufacturing Wage Determination Process." *Journal of Political Economy* 76 (September-October, 1968): 1015-36.

Ostry, Sylvia. "Interindustry Earnings Differentials in Canada, 1945-1956." *Industrial and Labor Relations Review* 12 (April, 1959): 335-52.

Pencavel, John H. "Wages, Specific Training and Labour Turnover in U.S. Manufacturing Industries." *International Labour Review* 13 (February, 1972): 53-64.

Raimon, R. L. "The indeterminateness of Wages of Semiskilled Workers." *Industrial and Labor Relations Review* 6 (January, 1953): 180-94.

Reder, M. W. "Wage Structure and Structural Unemployment." *Review of Economic Studies* 31 (October, 1964): 309-22.

Rosen, Sherwin. "On the Interindustry Wage and Hours Structure." *Journal of Political Economy* 77 (March/April, 1969): 249-73.

———. "Unionism and the Occupational Wage Structure in the United States." *International Economic Review* 11 (1970): 269-86.

Rosenbluth, G. "Wage Rates and the Allocation of Labour." *Canadian Journal of Economics* 1 (August, 1968): 566-82.

Schweitzer, S. O. "Factors Determining Interindustry Structure of Wages." *Industrial and Labor Relations Review* 22 (January, 1969): 217-25.

Slichter, Sumner H. "Notes on the Structure of Wages." *Review of Economics and Statistics* 32 (February, 1950): 80-91.

Vietorisz, Thomas and Bennett Harrison. "Labor Market Segmentation: Positive Feedback and Divergent Development." *American Economic Review* 63 (May, 1973): 366-76.

Williamson, Oliver E. "Wage Rates as a Barrier to Entry." *Quarterly Journal of Economics* 82 (February, 1969): 85-116.

Theses

Behman, Sara A. "Wage Determination in a Cyclical Setting." Ph.D. Thesis, University of California, Berkeley, 1966.

Chernick, S. E. "Studies in the Structure of Canadian Wages." Ph.D. Thesis, Massachusetts Institute of Technology, 1956.

Cohen, Malcom Stuart. "The Determinants of the Relative Supply and Demand for Unskilled Workers." Ph.D. Thesis, Massachusetts Institute of Technology, 1967.

Lutz, Mark Andreas. "The Equilibrium Industrial Wage Structure: An

Analysis in Terms of Wage Theory." Ph.D. Thesis, University of California, Berkeley, 1972.

Mulvey, Daniel. "A Study of Competing Theories of Interindustry Wage Structure Variation." Ph.D. Thesis, Georgetown University, 1965.

Reber, S. R. "The Effects of Unionism upon Relative Wages." Ph.D. Thesis, University of Chicago, 1970.

Ripley, Frank C. "The Structure of Wages in United States Manufacturing Industries, 1948-1964." Ph.D. Thesis, Harvard University, 1969.

Wachter, Michael L. "Relative Wage Determination Among Industries: Some Theoretical and Empirical Results." Ph.D. Thesis, Harvard University, 1970.

Working Papers

Hamermesh, Daniel S. "Inter-dependence in the Labour Market." Industrial Relations Section, Princeton University, Working Paper Series No. 32, November, 1971.

Johnson, G. E. "Non-Linearities in the Labor Market Adjustment Process." Princeton University, Systems Analysis of the Labour Market Working Paper Series No. 3, 1967.

Peitchinis, S. G. "The Canadian Industrial Wage Structure." University of Calgary, Department of Economics, Discussion Paper Series No. 2, October, 1970.

Rees, A. "Compensating Wage Differentials." Industrial Relations Section, Princeton University, Working Paper No. 41, January, 1973.

Government Material

Department of Consumer and Corporate Affairs. *Concentration in the Manufacturing Industries of Canada.* Ottawa: Information Canada, 1971.

Labour Canada, Economics and Research Branch. *Wage Rates, Salaries and Hours of Labour.* Ottawa: Information Canada, Annual.

———. *Working Conditions in Canadian Industry.* Ottawa: Information Canada, Annual.

Statistics Canada. *Manufacturing Industries of Canada.* Catalogue No. 31-203. Ottawa: Information Canada, Annual.

———. *Employment, Earnings and Hours.* Catalogue No. 72-002. Ottawa: Information Canada, Monthly.

———. *1961 Census of Canada.* Ottawa: Queen's Printer.

U.S. Department of Labor, Bureau of Labor Statistics. *Hand Book of Labor Statistics, 1971.* Bulletin No. 1705. Washington, D.C.: U.S. Government Printing Office.